WELL WORTH WAITING FOR

An Adoptees Story.

John Sheen

authorHOUSE®

AuthorHouse™ UK Ltd.
1663 Liberty Drive
Bloomington, IN 47403 USA
www.authorhouse.co.uk
Phone: 0800.197.4150

© 2014 John Sheen. All rights reserved.

No part of this book may be reproduced, stored in a retrieval system, or transmitted by any means without the written permission of the author.

Published by AuthorHouse 03/24/2014

ISBN: 978-1-4918-9736-2 (sc)
ISBN: 978-1-4918-9735-5 (hc)
ISBN: 978-1-4918-9737-9 (e)

Any people depicted in stock imagery provided by Thinkstock are models, and such images are being used for illustrative purposes only.
Certain stock imagery © Thinkstock.

This book is printed on acid-free paper.

Because of the dynamic nature of the Internet, any web addresses or links contained in this book may have changed since publication and may no longer be valid. The views expressed in this work are solely those of the author and do not necessarily reflect the views of the publisher, and the publisher hereby disclaims any responsibility for them.

Dedicated to the memory of
My Mum and Dad.

With thanks to
My Mother and Father for the gift of life.

To my brother Sid
Well worth finding.
Best wishes
John.

Introduction

I have included in this story various letters, photographs and copy certificates. This is in order to give a fuller understanding of exactly what transpired, and when, during my adoption process. Copies of some original letters were faded and in poor condition, and they have been re-typed.

It is only through those pages, found in my file, that I have understood myself. I hope it will be of some benefit, and give some understanding, to any adoptee who has little or no knowledge of their own journey.

I have been extremely fortunate in my own journey, mainly due to the parents who adopted me and brought me up. I am also fortunate to have found my birth families, and learn from them who knew my birth parents, what I have inherited from them.

Even with all the love and care which was showered upon me by my adoptive parents and grandparents, I still felt different. Once I was told what adoption meant, and that I had come from some other place, there was never a true feeling of belonging.

Finding my birth families has changed my life. I have a sense of belonging with them. I have a place in history that I never thought I would have, and I am able to bring my children, grandchildren, and great-grandchildren there. I have now got a past.

For clarity, throughout this story, I have referred to my adoptive parents as Mum and Dad, which is what I always called them. My biological parents I refer to as Mother and Father.

My journey has been difficult at times, and truly joyous at others. It has been exciting, and also unbelievably emotional.

There is one thing for certain . . . . it was well worth waiting for.

PROLOGUE

August 20th 1942. 10 15 am.

The train which had made possible the earliest connection with the Isle of Wight ferry at Portsmouth Harbour, pulled into Waterloo Station only a little late.

Amongst the throng of people, service men and women, nurses, and those still engaged in business amidst the middle of a world war, two women alighted from one of the carriages. The first was a slim young woman of twenty-eight wearing a brown felt hat and a yellow coat, the second a rather portly, matronly woman dressed in navy blue. The younger woman looked nervous but happy as she slipped her hand through the other woman's arm. The older woman looked more confident. They made their way to the ladies' waiting room where, outside, a woman on the short side wearing a fawn coat and a brown straw hat enquired as to the newcomers' names. Identities were exchanged.

The brief formalities over, they entered the waiting room. There sat a middle aged woman clutching in her arms a four month old baby boy. The young woman sat down and unbuttoned her coat in readiness to hold the child who, from this moment, was to be her son.

Far away in Long Eaton, near Nottingham in the middle of England, an ailing young woman, still exhausted from childbirth, was on the one hand full of remorse and guilt, and on the other, thankful that the decision she had made would probably save her marriage and reunite her with her first born son. She knew where her new-born was going, and was as certain as she could be that the child would be brought up as well as she would have liked to do herself, had circumstances been very different.

I am that child, and this is my story.

*   *   *

I was an ordinary nine year old child, enjoying the morning play-time at an ordinary village school, when my cousin came over to me and told me that my Mum and Dad were dead and that I was adopted. It couldn't be true, I knew, because they were both there when I left for school less than two hours ago. She was so insistent, that I ran the half mile home in fear.

I found my Mum at the kitchen sink! I was so thankful that things appeared absolutely normal, that I could only ask what "adopted" meant. My fear that what I had been told was true no longer concerned me, but I had asked a question which needed to be answered. What did "adopted" mean?

My Dad was immediately summoned from his work nearby, and I was made to sit in the living room for what must be an important explanation. I was asked where I had heard the word, and who had said it to me. My Mum, I can remember, was absolutely distraught and weeping. My Dad explained to me that he and Mum couldn't have a child unless one came from somewhere else, and that I had been especially chosen to be their little boy. That made me extra special. That was what "adopted" meant, and that I was no different to either of my cousins, my friends or my school mates. Even my Mum's dad, my grandfather, was adopted, and my Mum's favourite aunt too.
That's how special it was to be "adopted".

I don't doubt that all would have been explained to me at some time, at what would be considered the right time. I'll never know when that time was supposed to be, and in many ways it was probably a good thing that it had happened now. At nine years old I knew nothing about where babies came from. Maybe most were chosen from some place like I was. I had my Mum and Dad, who loved me. They had chosen me and had chosen my name. Of course I was theirs! I felt grown up, having completely accepted and understood what I was told.

I presume that my adoption had been discussed and likely overheard at my cousin's home, and also that she had been warned never to raise the subject with me again. She never did during our childhood, although there were instances when I was made to feel somewhat the outsider. That didn't worry me in the least, as my interests were completely different from my cousin's and I was, I suppose, a bit of a loner.

Throughout my early childhood, after I knew that I was adopted, although not really understanding, I did feel different. My aunt, and uncle and cousins lived in the village and were my nearest relatives other than my Mum, Dad, and grandparents. It was a big family on my Mum's side. My grandmother had brothers and sisters living on the Island. All had children much older than me.

Occasionally I was taken to visit the "aunts", and I felt somehow that I was on show. I knew that they knew that I came from somewhere else. I saw my grandmother's two brothers regularly at grandfather's workshop, where they were both employed. I got on well with them. Uncle Bill was a keen snooker player, and sometime later, he gave me a very nice cue, complete with spare tips and chalks, when I started to play myself. Uncle Jack was very musical and always whistling. He had a daughter who's singing he was very proud of. He himself was an excellent glazier, and was known as "Putty" My grandfather's sister was a great favourite of mine, and my Mum's favourite aunt. She had been adopted, as was my grandfather, but I knew nothing of their past history. Since that day when I first heard the word "adopted" it was never again mentioned, at least not within my hearing.

There were few relations on my Dad's side, just one uncle, Tom, who visited during my youth. He was a great tease and used to wind me up. He knew he could annoy me by calling me "titty baby" One day when I was about six, he arrived with a present. It was a huge pink sugar dummy. I was horrified, and accused him of stealing it from some baby's pram. The very worst and horrible thing I could think of to get my own back, was to call him a "rat with glasses". He never forgot it, and we laughed about it for years to come.

Most of his working life was spent at sea, as a chief chef on the White Star Line. This was after the "Titanic" disaster. In truth, as I found out much later, he wasn't Dad's brother at all, but his uncle. Dad was the illegitimate child of his uncle's sister. He was brought up by his grandparents, who he called Mum and Dad. I don't recall ever meeting them, and I don't know if my Dad ever knew his real mother. To have any of this come up in conversation in front of me would only draw attention to things that I wasn't supposed to know.

We lived almost next door to grandfather's building yard and workshop, and I spent many hours playing about there, and watching the men at work. It was said that enough wood off-cuts, and wire nails to build a house went down the river as part of the model boats I crudely constructed. The early years and the surroundings were truly joyous for a little boy, and being on my own suited me, although I was probably spoilt, just a bit. Before I had my own boat I could hardly wait for the tide to rise so that I could watch the commercial and pleasure craft on the river. I knew all the barges, yachts and motor boats by name. When I had my dinghy I would row over to anyone going sailing or fishing, just to say "Hello", and hope for an invitation to join them. My parents knew where I was, owing to whose mooring my dinghy was tied to.

In 1951, what I considered to be a very special looking yacht took up a mooring just off the yard. This was the sleekest, fastest looking boat I had ever seen. Called "Fortuna" and finished in a lovely shade of pale blue, it was the British entry in the Star Class for the 1952 Olympics being held in Helsinki. Of course I could only witness the picking up and dropping off of the mooring, as the training was carried out on the Solent and at Cowes. I determined to have a boat like that one day.

Being of local interest the result of the Olympic Regatta was announced at the village school. I was disappointed and could hardly believe that "Fortuna" hadn't won a gold medal, but I alone heartily clapped the thirteenth place, much to the amusement of everyone present. The gold medal was won by the Italian crew.
Good job my grandmother wasn't there! She had taken against all Italians because she thought they had cheated in a Schneider Trophy contest which she had watched from Cowes seafront many years before. She often voiced her opinion of those "blessed I-talians."

International Star Class, crew hiking out.

There was a small Children's Home just along the road from where we lived. On a couple of occasions my Mum sent me along there to stay overnight. I didn't like the food or sleeping in a crowded room, although the staff were kind and the children were very nice. There were about a dozen children resident there and I went to school with most of them. I didn't understand at all why I had to go to the Home. It wasn't as if my parents were away, and if they were I could have stayed with my grandparents.

Years afterwards I wondered if this was some kind of exercise to make sure I was happy and appreciative of my own home. Was I being shown what my situation would have been if I hadn't been adopted? Was I being shown that all these other children came from somewhere else just like me, and were absolutely normal? . . . . Except, of course, that they didn't have a Mum and Dad like me.

My childhood was on the whole very happy.
I wanted for nothing other than what I had or was given. It wasn't until I was a teenager that I came to realise that my parents actually had very little. My dad worked as a carpenter and joiner for my grandfather whilst Mum did part time work in the office. Our house belonged to my grandfather and rent was somehow worked off rather than actual money changing hands. There was always good food and I was clothed well.

I recall but two holidays together with my parents and their friends who owned a car.
They had a son of similar age to myself, and although we were not what would be called close friends, we got along together on these occasions and regularly met at Sunday school and youth club.

All my spare time was spent on the river which ran past the bottom of our garden and my grandfather's building yard and workshops.
Such was my interest in boats, that Dad had built me a small dinghy when I was six or seven. In my impatience waiting for the tide to rise I would push the dinghy across the mud until it floated.
One of my favourite pastimes was to wait for one of the cargo barges to be leaving and throw a line to one of the crew for a tow to where the river met the sea. I would then be cast off to row home.

As I grew older I of course began to understand adoption and the reasons for it, both from the giver's and the receiver's position. The matter was never again raised between my parents and myself. I understood that to enquire about my biological parents would only bring heartache to my Mum, who openly talked of "When she had me". I felt privileged to be where I was and felt no need to know anything further.

I did, at times, wonder why it was that I appeared to be the only member of my family, including uncles, cousins etc, who had this urge to be afloat. Other boys and girls from the village whose relations had boats were to be seen afloat in their company. I wondered whether my biological parents ever had a boat. I also wondered if either or both of them were keen athletes, as it was my passion during my school years, and I was fortunate to achieve some success even to county standard.

An amusing instance arose during what was, I suppose, my prime athletic period, aged thirteen or fourteen. A very close friend of my parents, who gave me some training, presented me with something he thought would be beneficial. I recall everyone's amusement, and my own embarrassment when I unwrapped a jock strap, declaring that I couldn't possibly be seen wearing just that at the championships!. Everyone else wore shorts.

The bearer of my gift, and my part time trainer, who I called "Uncle Don", had some influence on my life. He had been in the Royal Navy, and returning home on leave found his wife had run off with a soldier. He lodged with my parents for some time when I was very young and we spent many hours together.
He re-married when I was about six and moved to his own house. His new wife treated me as he did, and I began to wonder if he was in fact my real father and that his first wife could have been my mother.

Uncle and his new wife were both very regular visitors to our house, and I recall getting advice and encouragement from my "Uncle Don" more so than from my Dad. He moved away from the area in due course to a new job up north, but always sent me a birthday card with a short letter of encouragement in all I did. This to me was unusual as I would have expected his wife to write. My mum always did the letter writing from our house.

By the time I was about fifteen I had almost convinced myself that "Uncle Don" was my father, and I would have been pleased if it were so.

I never broached the subject to my parents or to my suspected father, and was happy to believe that I was right. I had two loving parents and perhaps another "dad" as well. Maybe time would tell . . . .

As for the identity of my biological mother, here again I had my own thoughts. I used to receive gifts at Christmas and birthdays from an "Auntie Margaret". Not a real auntie, not even a relative as far as I knew, but she never failed to send to me for many years. She never visited and I never met her, but she seemed to show great interest in me. She was not an old friend or school friend of either of my parents, and she periodically enclosed a photograph of herself in a greeting card. Dutifully I would reply to her cards with thanks, wondering just who she really was, and what was her possible connection with my parents and me.

Correspondence ended rather abruptly, and it was some time before my mother received a letter saying that my "Auntie Margaret" had stepped into an open lift shaft on the London Underground and been killed. Could this have been my real mum? I would probably never know now.

Despite having a happy childhood, there was a thought always lingering in the back of my mind that I was different . . . . different to my family in my interests, and different to some of my school friends who resembled in looks not only their siblings but also their parents.

There was one huge coincidence that confused me. At my grand-parents house hung a large engraving of my grand father's late father, my great grandfather of course. The likeness between us was, to say the least, noticeable to anyone.

Where then had I come from? Was this a genuine family likeness, and if it was so, why the great secrecy? I didn't ask.

I badly wanted to know from where I had come, but was too scared to ask. Asking would be the only solution, but I knew that to do so would only cause upset. Anyway, I could be no better off than I was, and the knowledge I sought could perhaps uncover things that were best forgotten.

John Sheen

My Mum almost seemed to forget that she had adopted me.
Repeatedly in conversation she would refer to "having me" and relate stories of my earliest days.

I caused great alarm at one time by asking for my birth certificate, sight of which was required by my school concerning a foreign trip to France. I was thirteen years old.
Whilst my class mates openly showed interesting certificates with information about their parents, mine was sealed in an envelope addressed to the head master. It was returned to me in like manner, addressed to my parents. It would, of course, have been my adoption certificate, not a birth certificate. No doubt there was a covering note explaining my ignorance of the matter.
While in France I used most of my pocket money to buy my Mum an enamel brooch depicting a pair of blue birds, which she treasured for many years.

As my school leaving days approached I had little idea of quite what I wanted to do, other than that I knew it should be something for myself. I had seen my Dad working for his father-in-law, my uncle working for the Council, and others in what could be termed regular work. I couldn't see any of them actually enjoying it.

I finally decided to learn Naval Architecture, so that I might design boats, and then perhaps build them. I thought it would be a fulfilling way of life. I was aware of the post-war boom in boating, and avidly followed the latest designs for both sailing dinghies and yachts. I had long given up weekly comics in favour of a monthly yachting magazine, and scrounged many back copies of other magazines from members of the local sailing club.

My plan didn't work out as I had hoped, as my mathematics were not good enough to pass the necessary exams to secure an apprenticeship. However, I was now determined to try my best to achieve my goal. I decided to learn boatbuilding first, and perhaps study the design aspect later.

I first started my boatbuilding whilst I was still at school.
I had done well at woodwork class, and had collected my tools over a period of time. I had been allowed space in my Dad's workshop, and had saved

from my wages as a Saturday morning butchers delivery boy. I purchased enough plywood and timber to build one or two pram dinghies which I sold through the local paper.
The dinghies were of simple construction, and the knowledge I had gleaned to build them had come from watching my Dad at work.
Far from discouraging me from my eventual chosen occupation, my Dad was inadvertently encouraging me.
My parents and grandparents had clubbed together for my thirteenth birthday and given me a second-hand ten foot sailing dinghy, on the understanding that the future maintenance was entirely down to myself. I did however get cans of paint for subsequent birthday presents. I did several alterations to the boat, and painted it a different colour each year.

My Mum made me promise that I would allow my cousins to use my boat, should they ask. Neither of them ever did. My original dinghy was stove in beyond repair, destroyed in fact. My cousin denied all knowledge of the incident, but it had been witnessed by one of my grandfather's employees. The sledge hammer, which had been taken from the store, was laid by the boat. I doubt she was punished by her parents.

My parents were not in favour of my choice of employment, pointing out that boatbuilding was not very secure. Most of the local yards had, on occasion, been on short time, and several local boat builders had from time to time been laid off.

My Dad especially, tried to encourage me to enter the building industry, but this didn't interest me at all. My great grandfather's firm built executive type houses, and was one of the biggest local companies. It was handed down to my grandfather, and finally to my Dad, by which time it employed only my Dad and one other, doing jobbing work and painting and decorating.

My grandfather was a lovely man, a staunch Methodist and Church organ player, but he was not a business man. Neither was my Dad. I knew he once had ambition and had wanted to emigrate to Canada or Australia, but my Mum wouldn't hear of it. I am sad that he lived most of his life in a kind of rut formed by marrying the boss's daughter.

Through a local self employed boat builder, with whom I had been spending weekends and evenings helping to rebuild a burnt out yacht, I learnt of a Cowes yard looking to take on an apprentice. I started my employment there a week before my sixteenth birthday.

I served three years of my apprenticeship at Cowes, mostly building small craft of a relatively new construction developed during the war. It was a light weight but very strong construction, but I became bored with the repetition of the work and wanted to learn more. I got on well with the boss and his brother who also worked there, and explained to them both how I felt. Soon afterwards I was summoned to the office and told that I could transfer my apprenticeship to a Bembridge yard still building traditional clinker motor boats and cruisers. My boss had arranged this for me and wished me good luck and success. I started there the following week, and enjoyed a variety of work for the next three years. After completing my apprenticeship I worked for one year earning a man's wage of eleven pounds per week. I was let go when a couple of chaps, who had worked there before, returned from National Service and took up their old jobs. I gradually set up on my own account with the help of more space in Dad's workshop and some sub contract work from both of my previous employers.

My "Coming out piece" when I completed my apprenticeship. Entirely built by myself and an apprentice.

My adoption had rarely been on my mind since leaving school, it wasn't a subject that ever arose amongst my work colleagues.
It obviously did cause me concern when I met my future wife. I was seventeen and she was sixteen. and we exchanged our family histories. She is from a long line of fishermen and longshoremen from the other side of the Island, and could trace her family back generations, even to smuggling days. I was fascinated by the stories not only she, but also that her grandfather, could tell. For my part I could only go back seventeen years.

The elder of my cousins approached my girl on a bus, and asked her if she knew that I had been adopted. She was horrified that he should have thought it was any of his business to tell her that I was adopted.

During a slack period in my boatbuilding I helped my Dad with some of his work. While we were painting the outside of a nearby semi-detached cottage, the owner, who had recently bought it as a development project, decided to sell. This was a golden opportunity for me. My girl and I had become engaged five years after meeting, but I would not agree a wedding date until we had our own house. This cottage would suit us splendidly. The problem was money. Apart from the purchase there was a great deal of work to be done to make it habitable.

We were very fortunate.

My prospective father-in-law loaned us the deposit, and the vendor, a woman from a landed gentry family offered us a mortgage. It took about a year to renovate the property and it was finished late on the night before our wedding, November 20th 1965. I was so proud to bring my wife home from honeymoon, and the fact that we were almost broke didn't matter. Our first week's housekeeping came in the form of a competition win waiting for my wife at her parent's home.
She had completely forgotten even entering.

My grandfather had sadly passed away in 1964. We had enjoyed his company on Sundays during his last years, when we would drive him in his old car which he could no longer manage himself. My future wife always fixed him up with a bib so as not to get ice cream on his best suit, and incur grandmother's good humoured wrath.

Just before our first son was born in 1968, my grandmother asked to spend an evening with my wife whilst I was to be out at a function. She was quite frail by this time and I had to collect her from her home about half a mile distant. During the night my wife had a nightmare. When she calmed down she said that my grandmother had asked her if she was concerned about the forthcoming birth, because I had been adopted. I don't think it was something we ourselves had even considered. We were both healthy, and my situation was accepted without concern. My grandmother obviously knew that I had never been told anything about my birth parents, and that I had never enquired. She, better than anyone, would understand why.

She thought that with the impending birth, and the fact that I knew nothing of my roots, she should know what there was to know about how I had arrived.

The first statement was that I had come from healthy stock. She went on to impart her full knowledge of the situation which had led to my adoption.

I came from London, and was collected during an air raid. My Mum and my grandfather's sister, her aunt, who was a midwife, had collected me. I was the second child of a soldier who had perished in a Japanese prisoner of war camp, and his wife. There was no information about my Mother, other than that I had to be adopted, presumably my two year old brother likewise.

My wife was unsure how to impart this news to me, and had decided to wait until morning to relate what she had been told.

The nightmare, and the calling of my name which had awakened me, depicted me in a Japanese P.O.W. camp being tortured.

After a few minutes she told me exactly what my grandmother had said. It is difficult to describe how I felt.

My first thoughts were of my Mother. Was she Auntie Margaret who had fallen down the lift shaft? Why had I been adopted? Couldn't my Mother look after me on her own? What happened to my brother? Where did he go? Why didn't he come with me, or be adopted nearby. so that we might get to know each other. Was my Father a hero? He had given his life for his country, but I would never know anything about him.

Then, of course, the questions started in my mind. Why was it all such a big secret until now? If I was going to learn the truth, then surely I had the right to know before. I was angry, but accepted that at least I knew now, and was grateful that I had been loved and brought up by a decent family.

One question had been settled. I now knew I was a Londoner. My red beard didn't come from Scotland, and I probably wasn't the descendant of a Viking. At least I wasn't Welsh.

I had a slight disliking of Welshmen following a school rugby game. I had successfully tackled the sports master, who was Welsh, much to his embarrassment in front of both teams.
He retaliated by giving me a painful kick in the testicles, for which I never forgave him. He put me right off Welshmen.

It was some considerable time before I stopped thinking, "What if this?" and "What if that?" There would be little point in questioning Mum and Dad, as they would know that my grandmother had brought things into the open. There was little else that could be said. I didn't want to show my anger, and waited to see if they would bring the subject up. They never did.

Accepting that my birth parents were dead, I nevertheless kept thinking about my brother. I wondered if he knew more than I did. Did he know about me? After all he was older and must have known our Mother, and possibly our Father.
There was no way I could find him, but would he perhaps try to find me? I had no idea. I found myself looking at men with red beards and of similar size and colouring, who were slightly older than me, just in case.

Then there was the etching of my great grandfather, and also the thoughts about Uncle Don. Nothing added up. All I could do was accept what I had, and be thankful.

We were starting our own family, my family. We might not have a past on my side, but would surely have a future.

Towards the end of 1968 my boatbuilding and associated crafts had expanded to the extent that the workshop didn't afford enough floor space for both mine and my Dad's needs.

The rear garden of our cottage backed onto an unmade road where there were a couple of commercial premises amongst a variety of houses and bungalows. I thought to construct a pre-fabricated building in which to carry out some of my work which didn't require the river frontage site. My planning application was refused. Shortly afterwards, a local developer made us an offer for part of the garden, stating that he was in negotiations to purchase part of my adjoining neighbour's garden. I discussed the matter with my Dad, who suggested that I should sell, and then extend the current workshop. The land upon which the workshop was built, extending to the river, belonged originally to my great grandfather and was now owned by my grandmother. We sold the top part of the cottage garden, which we had only once cultivated in an attempt to grow my pipe tobacco. The crop was once unsuccessfully raided in search of something more sinister than Virginia and Havana.

A pair of bungalows were subsequently approved for the developer.

The riverside workshop was extended and re-arranged to suit both my Dad and myself. The workshop was attached to the rear of my grandmother's house, which had been converted to residential use in the early 1950's from my great-grandfather's, and then grandfather's, machine and joiner's shop. This building had once produced all the timber parts for quality houses built between the wars. During the 1939-45 war the house building business was closed, but in his spare time from the shipyard, my Dad had made wooden toys which my Mum painted. They supplied Gamage's store in London. The current workshop and the river frontage was reached via a short driveway which ran between my grandmother's house and the semi-detached where my aunt and uncle had now moved to. Both cousins had now moved away. My parents lived in the other semi, but the whole plot, buildings and river frontage, were still owned by my grandmother . . . . or so I thought . . . .

Early in 1969, eight months or so after our first son was born, I attended a public meeting. It was called by The Crown Commissioners in order to outline a change of plan for the administration of the river foreshore in which they had a holding.

It was a similar proposal to that being sought in various parts of the country. The Crown would retain ownership, but the administration of moorings was to be handed over, by way of lease, to an elected body of river users and riparian owners. There was also the requirement to keep the fairway channel clear on behalf of the Queen's Harbour Master, Portsmouth. It was an amicable meeting, and well attended. When the meeting closed I took the trouble to inspect the various charts on display, and noticed that the land on which my workshop was built, together with a sizeable chunk of my grandmother's three properties was coloured in red.

I asked the representative of the Crown for an explanation.

I was told that the red area had been leased or rented to a private individual who appeared to have no further interest in the land, and that it would be sold on the open market. There was interest!

Following the meeting I went straight to my parents, and together we called on my aunt and my grandmother. Their properties belonged, of course, to my grandmother, but two were occupied by her daughters.
It transpired that there had been several letters from the Crown to my grandmother, the last as good as giving notice unless she wished to purchase. The matter had gone unheeded by all who should have been concerned.

There was certainly concern now.

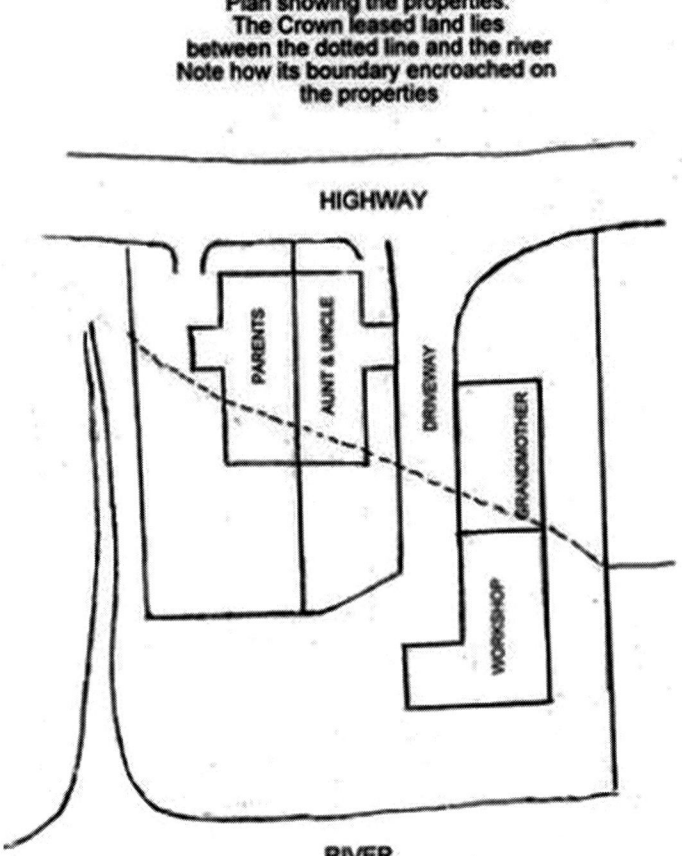

Plan showing the properties.
The Crown leased land lies between the dotted line and the river
Note how its boundary encroached on the properties

There was varied speculation as to who, among the local business men, speculators and developers might seize the opportunity to acquire water frontage. There was no family money available for the purchase, and I was persuaded that I should, if possible, buy the land.

My grandmother said she would reply to the last letter and request that I, her grandson, be permitted to make the purchase. All agreed that, as it was primarily my livelihood at stake, and that my age may enable me to raise the money, this would be a satisfactory solution.

A few weeks later I attended an appointment with my solicitor to peruse a draft contract. I explained the situation regarding the various properties, and asked that they be excluded from the land deed when registered, so that the three houses were legally separated and had their own boundaries. This also had to be considered when applying for a loan, if part of the whole was to be given away, or made over. My solicitor liaised with the family solicitor at my expense, and I obtained the necessary loan from my bank. Problem solved, or so I thought . . . .

Some time later my elder cousin paid a visit from the mainland and we briefly discussed what had been achieved. Immediately he was hostile. His father, my uncle, together with my parents, arrived at our house.
My uncle was furious. He shouted and raved, saying I had no right to buy all the land. I was an outsider and didn't belong. I was a bastard. This, of course, made my parents angry and there was an almighty row. I couldn't believe that anyone should take such an attitude, especially as the property in which he lived didn't belong to him, but to his mother-in-law.

From then on things just got worse.

I had to pass my aunt's back door going to and from my work, and I suffered disgusting verbal abuse from her husband. No doubt the whole village now knew that I had been born out of wedlock. That didn't worry me too much. Neither did his standing outside our front gate for ages on end waiting for the opportunity to vent his hate.

What was more worrying was that my wife and my Mum got similar treatment. Coal was thrown at my wife while she was wheeling our son's pram through the driveway. My Mum was scared to go into her garden. She was becoming estranged from her sister, and lived in fear of any encounter with her sister's husband.

My workshop was broken into. A new dinghy, ready to be dispatched, had a saw put through the gunwale and into the hull. It was impossible to repair the damage satisfactorily.

It was also impossible to prove anything without the police becoming involved. I didn't want my aunt to suffer further.

I left my workshop one dark evening, having doused the lights, and caught a movement from the shadows.
I managed to use my arm to fend off a shovel aimed at my head. My duffle coat, pullover and shirt were cut through. I entered the gateway, grabbed the shovel, disposed of it, and then opened the house door and threw this evil man into his kitchen. I then went straight to the police station.

The following day, after hanging from the bedroom window threatening to kill himself, he was arrested and then taken away in a straight-jacket by Social Services.

My aunt, and also my Mum, pleaded with me not to press charges if I received an apology, and the promise that there would be no further trouble. My aunt promised that they would move away as soon as possible. The police also warned that any other unreasonable behaviour would be treated as a second offence. The report from the mental hospital stated that my uncle was not mentally ill, but eaten up with hatred and jealousy.

In due course the house in which my aunt lived was valued. and allegedly did not equal the price of a desired bungalow.
For everyone's sake I accepted a token offer for a strip of land which afforded river access to the property, enhancing its value, and the house was sold. I never again saw my uncle, or my aunt, and only saw my cousins in passing.

My grandmother had passed away after being nursed by my Mum for a considerable time. Her estate was to be divided between her daughters. As my Mum wanted to keep the original workshop conversion, once lived in by my grandparents, and her own home, she was obliged to allow her sister to inherit the balance of the estate, just to keep the peace. My aunt did rather well out of the arrangement. My Mum was too easily satisfied, but not the type to bear a grudge.

The younger of my cousins had married and now lived only a few houses away from my wife and I. It would seem that she had some difficulty conceiving a child of her own.

She adopted a little boy.

How ironic! I wonder what her father thought of that!

My wife called with some clothes she had knitted for the new baby. They were thrown back at her with the comment that "they didn't need our filthy hand me downs."

All the previously mentioned trouble took a toll on both my parents and my wife and I.

Work had slowed up considerably and it wasn't easy to manage.
I was fortunate to get some sub contract work at another yard, and we also took in a summer foreign student.

By the time our second son was born in February 1970 we were having difficulty paying our mortgage. The lady who held the mortgage came to see us. She had heard of our family troubles, as most of the village had, and she offered to help.

We were too proud to ask for a break in our payments, but she said she would like to credit us with a month's mortgage payment as a gift for the new baby. This was a most generous offer and we accepted gratefully.

Slowly things picked up, and I was soon back at work. There was little boatbuilding, but other work came my way.
I did some model making for The British Hovercraft Corporation and also some for a film company. One job was to build a model hover track and hover train to depict what the future might hold. I laid 100 yards of track on pylons, and I pulled the train with a winch made from an upturned bicycle. The rate of pedal was geared to simulate 250 miles per hour.
The height of the field allowed a distant view of the Solent and the mainland shore. It was a very realistic film set.

It was while I was engaged with this contract that a local fisherman, who was actually an "honourable" with Royal connections, but a bit of a black sheep in his family, came roaring across the field on his old B.S.A. Bantam. He had come across an old bank account which he had forgotten about, and wanted me to build him a new netting boat.

He wanted a sixteen foot mahogany on oak, clinker built boat. My wife assisted in the building by holding on the nail heads while I clenched up. We had worked like this many times before.

The fishing boat, named "Two Brothers", was a success, and I made a mould for production in fibreglass. They were moulded and marketed by a local company, and I received a small royalty on each one produced. More than a few went out the back door, for which I received nothing. Later on I introduced an eighteen and a twenty footer, under the same arrangement. I didn't always get paid in money . . . . in fact I was obliged to accept a second hand car on two occasions, and some payment in materials, but it worked out somehow.

"Neptune Twenty"

One of the bigger jobs I undertook, entirely on my own, was a major alteration of a motor cruiser. This boat had a well designed hull, with fairly flat after sections and a fine bow.
With the right amount of power she could be quite a fast boat.
The hull and deck were quite sound, but the cabin top and wheelhouse were crude in design and construction, and rather ugly. The old side valve Morris Vedette engine only produced enough horsepower to gain about five knots.

My task was to redesign and build the cabin and wheelhouse in African mahogany, and re-engine the boat with a powerful inboard-outboard, complete with new fuel tanks and other necessary extras. The aim was to realise the full potential of the hull. My customer was a well known local pork butcher, with several shops and a wholesale outlet, known to all as "Porky".

Periodically while I was doing the work, my customer would make part payments as initially agreed, and would also bring me something from one of his shops, for instance a few pork chops, or a pack of bacon and some of his shop made sausages or pies.
This was a satisfactory arrangement, and continued until the work was completed.

I launched the boat, and we, the owner and I, conducted successful trials. Everything was in order.

We returned to the yard, and I asked if he would like to square up the account, which I had to hand, and take delivery. He had a jetty further up the river, where the boat was to be kept. He said he didn't think to bring his cheque book, and suggested we leave things to the morrow.

In the morning the boat was missing!!!

I soon discovered that the boat had been moved to my customer's jetty. It had probably been towed by a rowing boat so as not to make any noise. My parents would surely have been alerted by the sound of an engine in the middle of the night.

I didn't much like the way this had been carried out, but considered that, despite almost daily visits whilst the work was underway, it was reasonable to give a period of grace before submitting the account in case of any unforeseen problems.

I heard nothing at all, and sent the account a couple of weeks later. There was no response to this, nor indeed to the account rendered which I sent at the end of the month. The final demand was sent on a post card, with a red overdue stamp. The next morning I got a lot of abuse down my telephone.

"How dare you do this? I don't want the postman to know that I owe money". "There's one simple answer," I told him. "Pay your bill!". Nothing transpired for a few weeks, but the boat was being used on a regular basis.

One Saturday, which I knew to be a busy butcher's day, I went to the shop that he usually worked in. He was in the cubicle at the far end, taking the money according to the tickets issued by his counter staff. I joined a long queue of shoppers and when I got to the kiosk I put my upturned hand through the semi-circular opening at the bottom of the glass screen. He hadn't seen me coming. He turned red, then purple. "You can't come in here for money. Anyway I haven't got any here". I remarked that I had seen just about enough to pay my bill, going through the till. People were queued up behind me, and the staff were watching!

He was furious. He opened the till and got out his wallet, and counted out what I was owed in cash. The final remark was, "Don't you ever come in this shop again!"

A couple of years later, on a balmy summer evening, Porky's boat was coming up the river on a falling tide, and out of the channel. I remarked to my wife that he was very likely to run aground. Just as he got opposite us he ground to a halt.
His speed was such that he was firmly stuck and unable to reverse off. We watched owner and crew debating what to do. Porky was seen to remove his shoes and socks, roll up his trousers, and tentatively test the, by now shallow, water covering the thick black oozy mud.

I went to the bottom of the yard, clad in Wellington boots, and armed with a pair of oars. My dinghy was tied to the pontoon.
A cheery wave, and an "It would be worth something", was called to me. I pushed the dinghy across the mud and tied a stout line onto the nearest mooring, and then to the motor cruiser's bow.

I went alongside and Porky got in the stern of my dinghy, with his crew in the bow. As we rowed up the river, now quite narrow, Porky said, "I appreciate this, so what would you like for the weekend, a nice pork joint perhaps?" "No thank you" I replied. "I was put off pork a while ago, but I'd like a bloody great joint of beef". "But I don't sell beef", he said. "I know", I replied. "So buy me one".

I dropped them off at the public landing stage. The following Saturday morning there was a delivery to our house, of a fine joint of sirloin. The next time I saw him he said quite amicably, "You bugger!" and laughed . . . . So did I!

In 1972, six weeks before the birth of our youngest boy, I had a fight with a circular saw. Two fingers were hanging off, and I put my right forefinger in a matchbox. A friend drove me to the hospital. I was home in a couple of days, with fifty two stitches and some wire holding my hand together, but I had lost the use of my arm. The kickback from the wood I was cutting had damaged the nerves. I was unable to work. Once again things looked pretty desperate.

My wife was brought up in her parents' guest house, and had also earned qualifications in catering, so we decided to sell our cottage and buy a small guest house for ourselves. We worked out that the equity in our cottage might furnish the deposit for a guest house. We worked out how many rooms would be needed to cover the probable mortgage payments and provide an income. My job would be vacuuming and one handed washing up, as well as entertaining our boys. This meant a trip to the beach each day. I really was getting the easy bit!

Word had gone round the village, and we had buyers almost queuing for the cottage.

We found a property that seemed suitable in Ryde, and I phoned my bank manager. There was a phone call in the afternoon, and the bank manager said he had walked round to the guest house in his lunch hour, and thought it was well worth going ahead. His exact words were, "Go ahead and write the cheque whenever". Those were the days!

We sold the cottage and moved in June with a six week old baby and our two boys. Thanks to a couple of friends, armed with brushes, paint and rollers, the house was decorated in a week.

The guest house was full within a couple of weeks, and the business took off.

We met many nice people, families as well, and the local tourist office sent us many customers. We continued as planned for four years, but the work was hard on my wife. I became restless and needed to get my workshop back into use.

Mum asked us if we would be interested in purchasing grandmother's old house. After much thought we decided to move back to the village.
We still had an overdraft at the bank, as a mortgage was never arranged. When I called in at the bank to ask for a settlement figure, the manager embarrassingly said that the bank had never taken a charge. We did, however, pay off our loan when we sold the guest house.

We bought the old house from mum, and moved back in 1976. We settled once again to village life and life by the river.

An old customer called to see me to enquire about a new boat, but I didn't think I could oblige because I hadn't regained full use of my arm. He wrote a cheque, and asked if I could build it for that amount. If I could, I should bank the cheque and let him know when the boat was ready. There was no hurry.

I built his boat for the amount on the cheque, and many others over the next few years. At one time I had eight employees but normally it was two or three. We built three boats for Jack Hargreaves, of the Southern T V "Out of Town" programmes, and also exported fishing boats to France. I appeared on television with Jack Hargreaves a couple of times, and he introduced me as "My old friend John Sheen". The publicity was certainly beneficial to my business.

In late1976 we decided to take a holiday. My wife had always wanted to visit Scotland. We had, at that time, an old Range Rover, so there was plenty of room for us as a family.
We decided on a central location, and eventually chose Callander, where the "Dr Finlay's Casebook" T V series had been filmed.

On our way north we stayed for a night at my Uncle Don's in Ormskirk, Lancashire. His wife had been ill, and we hadn't seen them for a couple of years. They generally visited the Island every year, and their two daughters, when young, loved to come. They also had a son Paul who was now nine years old.

We asked if Paul would like to accompany us on our holiday, as he hadn't been anywhere that summer owing to his mother's ill—health. Our boys were very excited, it would be like having a big brother along.

We arrived at Callander in the early evening, and there in the hotel car park was a car from our village. I knew the owner quite well. I also knew the husband of the woman retrieving the luggage from the boot. They were not one and the same. I've often heard the expression "not in your own back yard", but they were hundreds of miles away! Our Range Rover was obviously well recognised in the village, and would be known to the couple.

In the morning, they had disappeared. They had suddenly checked out. They need not have worried. None of our business!

We occupied a double and a family room. The hotel was very comfortable, and the breakfast was excellent. On our first morning my wife asked to use the laundry facilities situated in the basement. She arrived at the washing machines only to find her packet of soap powder was empty.
On retracing her steps, she found a trail of powder up two flights of stairs, and along the landing. Not a good impression to start with, but it caused no problem.

We toured all around, marvelling at the wonderful scenery, and visiting quaint little fishing villages. At Tarbert, Loch Fyne, we were walking along the quay when we almost collided with Bill and Vera Waight, friends of ours from home. Neither of us had any idea the others were coming to Scotland. Bill hadn't driven up, they and their car travelled by train. I hadn't thought of doing that myself, in fact I didn't know it could be done.
Bill was very knowledgeable about the area, as he had managed a boatyard there in the past. He was able to show us one or two of the fishing boats that were built in the yard to his design.

John Sheen

We usually ate our main meal at lunch time, and had a picnic tea amongst the heather at the end of the day. This gave all the boys time to use up any surplus energy, and guaranteed an early night for them. We could keep an eye on them between our drinks at the hotel bar.

We paid a visit to a customer of mine in Ayr, Mr Alistair Mackay. He had taken several of my fibreglass hulls over a period, and fitted them out for his local customers. It was interesting to see some of my work converted by some of his. The wooden boats that he built were of the type used in Orkney, from where he had originally set up business.

He had moved to Ayr to make transport easier and open up a bigger market. He always collected his hulls from me on a trailer, towed by his Mk 10 V 12 Jaguar. He thought the comfort far outweighed the cost, and he saved time by having a fast car.

While we were there, he ordered another twenty foot hull from me, and paid a cash deposit in recognition of a discount.
Little did we know then how useful that would be.

On our journey back down to Ormskirk, the clutch went on the Rover. The screeching noise was deafening. We had to take it very carefully, but we made our destination.
It took two days to get the car fixed. Yet another cash transaction! There was nothing of the boat deposit left!

I managed to find an old Star Class yacht, not as good as "Fortuna" of Olympic fame, but a nice boat all the same.
She was built in Monaco for the 1948 Olympics. (No result known). I did some restoration, and with my wife as crew, we raced in the local yacht club under handicap rules. We had some great sails, and some amusing times too. Our mooring was at the top of the river, but the yacht club was at the bottom. One day we were a bit late getting under way, and there was hardly a breath of wind. I thought we should miss our starting gun.
The local driving instructor motored by in his boat, and offered a tow out. This was quickly accepted.

No sooner had he made fast our line and got under way, than the breeze suddenly picked up from aft. We bore down on the outboard motorboat, and began to overtake. The poor chap began to panic, and couldn't undo his knots. We were now sailing at some speed, and ended up towing the outboard boat backwards. It was like a tug of war, until I managed to cut the line. He was then motoring in the wrong direction, but we made the start.

On another occasion we were racing into the harbour where we had to round a buoy and then cross the finish line.
It was a glorious week end and the harbour was packed with fine yachts moored up for a rally. We were, as our handicap allowed, well in the lead, although slower boats could well beat us on corrected time.
In the old days, these Star boats were sailed with the helmsman and crew lying along the deck with one knee draped over the topside. To be honest, we were showing off. Suddenly my corduroy clad knee dragged in the water and pulled me off.
My crew still looking forward had no idea what had happened, and wondered why people were shouting "pull him in"
I still had hold of the main sheet, and each time I tried to pull myself aboard, I hardened up and the boat heeled further over.
All the time we were bearing down on these luxury yachts, completely out of control. At last, in one final effort, I got back on board, swung around the buoy and got the finishing gun.

Later when we went down to the club to sign out, a chap came over to congratulate us. No need to rub it in I thought, but he was deadly serious. "I've seen some sailing in my time" he said, "but you were standing on the keel to keep her upright. Bloody marvellous" He wouldn't have it any other way. But I learnt a lesson. No showing off, and no corduroys afloat. 1977 was a good year for us. The summer weather was not particularly kind, but we did lots of boating.

I had built for ourselves one of the Grand Banks dories of which I had sold quite a number. This was used as a demonstrator and yard boat. It was fitted with a small Seagull outboard motor.

John Sheen

June saw the Spithead Fleet Review, marking the Queen's Silver Jubilee, and Spithead was crowded with all the Royal Navy could muster.

I painted the boat red, white and blue, and hoisted a huge Union Flag up a temporary mast. The five of us, plus the dog and picnic hamper, spent the day going round the fleet, viewing the ships.

There were a great many other spectators in a variety of pleasure craft, and we must have had our photographs taken as many times as the Royal Yacht Britannia. It was a great day.

Most weekends we were afloat. One of our favourite places was Priory Bay. The dory was of very shallow draught, and we could sail or motor right onto the beach. Although not really a sailing boat, we used a huge beer garden umbrella as a sail when the wind was behind us.

We also used to go spinning for mackerel on evening tides. The boys would watch for gulls swooping on the whitebait that the mackerel drove to the surface. Our house was very popular for mackerel suppers when the pub cleared out. I would take the spare from the catch there, if we had more than we needed, and exchange a few for a pint or two.

I also had a couple of old lobster pots, and a worn out trammel net which I sometimes set for crabs. My wife would dress them, and sell them around the village. Being a fisherman's daughter, and watching her mother dress crabs all her early life, she was an expert at it. Not wishing to look like a fishwife though, she always wore her best when hawking crab.

I once netted a large sea trout, and poached it in port. We invited some friends to join us for supper. It was delicious.

One of the most interesting jobs I had in my workshop, was the construction of an experimental aeroplane. It was built of aircraft plywood and Spruce, and covered in fabric. It was powered with a modified V.W. engine

Well Worth Waiting For

It wasn't often that I thought about the fact that I was adopted. It was always there in the back of the mind, ready to stir in response to a comment or something on the television or the radio.

I was resigned to the fact that I knew all I would ever know, and did that really matter? I didn't think so, until, that is, I was serving on a local committee, and got to know a chap who worked on the bridge on the river Kwai. He had experience of the Japanese camps. I told him of my known past, as related to my wife by my grandmother, and he was very interested. He belonged to a Veterans' Association of some kind, and said I might be able to get information about my father. The problem was, where to start without a name?. My grandmother was no longer with us, so that left only my parents. I could not bring myself to chance any upset.

I presumed my parents realised that I was happy with my lot, and I had never asked about my adoption, or put them in a position that I knew would upset them. We got on pretty well, and they were proud of their grand-children, and, I suppose, proud of us as parents.

I remember the morning after our first was born, I called to see my old boatbuilding friend to tell him of the birth. "I know", he said. "Christopher John, eight pounds, ten ounces. Born at a quarter to eight last night. Your Dad was up the road this morning, shouting it out".

Yes, they were proud.

Many times my wife and I discussed whether there might be a way to find out about my past, without involving Mum and Dad.
My wife was not in favour. We had no idea if it was possible even. What if there were things in my past that we wouldn't want to know? Was it worth chancing the possible upset? It was possible that there was nobody who would want me to turn up, and if there was, would the intrusion be welcome? We reached the same conclusion every time. Leave well alone for now.

There was a time when it appeared to me that everything would be laid bare, and it was instigated by my Dad.

He had always been slightly interested in fishing, but suddenly it became a regular hobby, with night-time outings. On one of his fishing nights out I was amazed, and somewhat taken aback, when I walked into a not-too-frequently visited pub, and there sat my Dad with a woman. Obviously embarrassed, he tried to ignore me.

A few days later he told me that his lady friend, for whom he had been doing some decorating, was a partner in an infertile marriage, but she didn't think she was responsible. My Dad had explained that he was in a similar marriage. Coincidentally, she and her husband had also adopted. My Dad and his "lady friend" both wanted to know if they were capable of reproducing. It seems that the affair had been going on for some considerable time, and although I only ever saw one five pound sea bass, I learned that they had, between them, netted a couple of bambinos.

I thought that this revelation would somehow expand into some explanation of my past, but it didn't. What I found very sad was that, apparently, my Mum knew of the goings on. Surely she didn't approve? It wasn't my place to interfere. Maybe, just maybe, if I was their son, and not by adoption, then I would have had it out with him. You just can't know your own parents, especially if you have been adopted by them. The genes are different.

Everything calmed down after a while and, although I loved these parents, I didn't understand them. I needed to know about my other parents.

The V A T rate on luxury goods, including boats, of 25% imposed by Labour's Dennis Healy in 1974, was disastrous.
This high rate had seen many small yards and manufacturers go out of business, never to return.

We were, at this time, running the guest house so the boat work wasn't so important, but I still had the workshop. When we had moved back to the village we completely re-furbished the house. We converted the attached garage into a dining room, and the store above was turned into a lounge with picture windows overlooking the river.

The end of the seventies and early eighties, however, saw a revival in general for boatbuilding, and we became involved in fund raising for the British challenge for the America's Cup.
My wife had, for a period, worked at a local company which made canvas goods, boat covers, flags and similar marine merchandise. We put together a package in support of the challenge.

We purchased an industrial sewing machine and designed a burgee which could be sold to supporters at promotional events nationally. I produced half hull scale models of the challenger "Lionheart", mounted on a mahogany plaque. We supplied the "Friends of Lionheart" team and they made a handsome profit. The London International Boat Show sold out of burgees on the first day, and we were sending as many as we could make in a day up to London each morning. The half models were to order only, and I produced many.

Unfortunately the challenge was not successful. We again became involved with the America's Cup of 1987 which was being held in Australia. I had developed a mini keelboat based on the "Lionheart" design. Through a contact made at Australia House, I secured a sponsored event to run in conjunction with the Cup itself. This would involve six of my boats, all in liveries of the competing nations. They would be sailed in a series of worldwide televised races. The event was to be sponsored by a soft drinks "real thing" company, and the Western Australia Tourism Commission. My negotiated fee was a big one. A builder was appointed in Perth, and new moulds were made and air freighted out. They didn't arrive on schedule, or indeed at all. This spelt big trouble for us.

With the help of the Western Australian Government through my London contact, the moulds were eventually found in Karachi, locked in an airport store. No one had any idea how this could have come about. The Tourism Commission arranged delivery to Perth. The problem now was that time was running out and we were in danger of being sued by the other sponsors.

This had now become a matter beyond my control, and needed some legal input. My solicitor had by now retired, and I was obliged to go elsewhere. The airline was soon contacted and made aware of the situation. There was no time to get the boats built by my builder in Perth, as he was not familiar with the boat. It was decided that I should somehow get to Perth and try to salvage what I could. The airline offered a return ticket on a flight leaving two days ahead, and faxed a covering letter of apology. The problem now was that I had an out of date passport, and I also needed a visa. Once again Australia House came to the rescue. They arranged my passport and my visa, all within the day. I travelled to London by train that evening, and at the back door of the Tourism Commission I gave the agreed password to the night security. I flew out the following day not quite knowing how things might turn out.

This was only the second time I had flown, and I was nervous.
However, I decided to make the most of the situation, and showing my copy letter signed by the airline chairman, I asked the steward if this would entitle me to a visit to the cockpit.
Within minutes I was sitting in the co-pilot's seat of a jumbo jet looking down on The Philippines, an experience I shall never forget. I arrived in Perth in the early hours of the morning. I hesitated to call my builder at such an early hour, and when I eventually did, it was to find that he had not received any notice of my arrival. Not a good start at all.

I was picked up with all my gear, including a few suits of sails and various other items which I hoped would save time in completing my obligations.

It was going to be an impossible task to put on the Mini America's Cup event using my boats, as originally intended.

Several meetings were held at the P R company involved, and it was eventually agreed that I should supply two completed boats. They were to be in the livery of the eventual defender and challenger in The America's Cup, which would be determined by the knockout races which were already well underway.

This at least was some relief, but my fee was now virtually non existent. My only hope was to get as much publicity as possible and market my boats. I had already had enquiries from New Zealand and the United States, from prospective licensed builders.

My accommodation at the boat builders I had selected as my Western Australian licensee, was, to say the least, basic. On the day of my arrival a few sheets of corrugated iron were erected around the front porch of their house, and this was my office and bed-sit. Not ideal, but I'm sure my hosts did their best for me. The family, a husband, wife and two sons, were really nice people, and we got along fine.

I constructed two boats as agreed. The materials required were supplied by my builder. I myself had little finance available, and could only supply the necessary labour.

It was about six weeks before I knew the correct colours for the boats, and they were not standard by any means. We constructed a trailer to house both boats, side by side, and I took them down to Fremantle to the American "Stars and Stripes" compound. They had won the right to challenge, and the "Kookaburra" was to defend The Cup. Both boats were sprayed for me at no charge, one dark metallic blue, the other gold and green. They both looked splendid. I was now able to fulfil my scaled down obligations. I was out of money, but out of trouble. Or was I?

Australia lost the series, and The Cup would now return to America. The weeks of hype on television and in the press, and what seemed to be the whole of Western Australia, went absolutely dead. It was unbelievable. I had my boats on a loaned pontoon, but as the Cup people left, there was little interest. It was time to pack up and fly home. I had no money left and I knew things at home were difficult.

I had become rather embarrassed, being a non-paying guest of my hosts. I now had little prospect of setting up a worthwhile business with them.

I had several relaxing week ends with a friend who had emigrated to Perth a few years before. The times spent with him and his wife allowed me some relief from my worries particularly concerning the situation at home. We were now in danger of losing the house unless things improved rapidly. I had already decided to leave my boats with the builder in payment for his hospitality. It would help to make up for the disappointment of what appeared to be a failed business opportunity.

I went to a travel agent to arrange a flight home. I showed my return ticket, and the outcome of the conversation between the agent and the airline, was that my ticket had been withdrawn. Frantic phone calls to the U K eventually discovered that my solicitor had commenced action against the airline, and that had caused the ticket withdrawal.

I was stuck.

I went to the Immigration Office to enquire about extending my visa, which appeared to cover only the period I had expected to be in the country. It took a couple of hours of telephone calls and faxes between Perth and London to clarify the situation. I was told that I could not be asked to leave the country, and that I was covered to work. This wasn't much help to me. I spent most days down at Fremantle with the boats, and although I wasn't licenced to hire them out, especially as I was situated just below the harbour master's office, I had plenty of people asking to hire. I could only tell them that I was not licensed to hire, but that I hadn't eaten that day, and they could go for a sail if they bought me a meal. It worked quite well, and I found a few dollars left in the boats.

There was, and probably still is, a fish and chip shop called Cicerello's in Fremantle, by the harbour, and the portions were huge. I sometimes took up station nearby and watched customers at the outside tables, who couldn't manage their meal.

I raided the waste baskets almost on a daily basis.

I was pretty much out of control by now, and having difficulty in thinking straight.

A long weekend with my friends, whose parents were out from home and seriously considering emigrating themselves, gave me food for thought. I had met many people in the marine business, and learned a lot about boating in Australia. Perth in particular, is very English, and there are areas and streets named after places back on my island.

I spent a couple of weeks looking into the possibility of returning in the not too distant future with my family.

I was offered a partnership with an ex pat who was setting up a marine business, and it seemed entirely feasible, provided I could prove the right qualifications for the job, which had to be advertised firstly to Australians.

John Sheen

I was asked to write the job description to suit my own experience. There was no problem.

The employment situation here in Western Australia was far better than back home, wages were better compared to the cost of living, and property prices were affordable.
I made enquiries on behalf of my wife and three sons regarding employment, and was greatly encouraged by the responses I received. There was no doubt in my mind that Australia was indeed a land of opportunity, and after talking to my wife and boys, and a few hasty letters, we agreed that a fresh start would be good for us.

I managed to secure a few weeks work with a small firm making fibreglass garage doors which kept me fed, and allowed time for us all to reflect on the proposal.
Every one that I met, mostly through my friends, were full of encouragement. I sold one of my boats to my prospective partner, the other I gave to my boatbuilding family. Hardly enough, as I had hoped to leave both boats with them, but I now had the means to get home after almost seven months. It had been very hard at times, and most enjoyable at others, I hoped the future would favour the enjoyable.

I arrived home without warning, because the telephone had been cut off. I had just over three pounds to my name, but that didn't matter. I was home at last with my family, and now it was time to get things sorted.

When I called in to Mum and Dad's, I was shocked to find that their health had suffered while I was away. I think the climax came because we were going to leave them. Dad pretended to be all for it. As I mentioned previously, he once had ambitions to emigrate. Mum, on the other hand, begged us not to leave them and take their grandchildren. They would never see us again.
I felt somewhat ashamed that I was causing so much grief to these people who had brought me up as their own, cared for me, and loved me all my life. We couldn't just walk away and leave them.

Our first money came in the form of a cheque from the Council. They had made an error in calculating our rates, which my wife had managed to pay by selling grandmother's antique cabinet. We got the money back, but the cabinet was lost. Not that we could have eaten it anyway, so never mind.

Somehow we managed to keep going all that summer by selling things at car boot sales. My wife had my Dad's greenhouse full of plants which she had brought on, and I made trellis panels and rose arches, which I took orders for. We forgot Australia.

We had plans drawn up for developing part of the boat yard. The application was initially refused, but finally approved by a single vote, despite letters of objection from my cousin's family and friends.

Would they never give up.?

My bank had said that they would finance the development if we received approval, and I was soon in the manager's office clutching my drawings, and the Approval Certificate. He said he would be in touch shortly.

Several weeks went by with no contact, and in the mean time there was a charging order put on the land by an impatient creditor. It was actually a false claim which led to the order. My wife couldn't handle it while I was abroad, and I had foolishly ignored it on my return.

I contacted the bank and made an appointment with the manager.
In his office he told me that the bank would not now be prepared to provide finance. He personally was "very sorry", but, "just between you and I, and these four walls, you are going to lose the land. I know who will get it, and what saddens me most is that I am obliged to supply the finance". "Not bloody likely", I thought, and went straight to an estate agent I knew, who didn't roll his trouser leg up, and asked him to find a quick buyer.

Fortunately my agent already had someone, from the Mainland on his books, seeking a plot with water frontage. Contact was made, and details forwarded. We received an offer, which we had no alternative but to accept. The planning approval was for two fisherman's cottage type properties, and the interested party stated that his sister would be interested in the second plot.

I had by this time changed solicitors again, and gave instructions to him. It was now a race between securing a sale and having the land auctioned. My solicitor seemed very tardy in furnishing a contract, and advised me to give up. It was not long before an auction date was fixed, to be held at a public house in town. My land was the only lot.

Purely by chance, a friend invited me to accompany him to the mainland, where he introduced me to his own lawyer.
With nothing to lose, I explained my situation, and sought the man's opinion. The latest situation was that the auction was in a week's time, and my solicitor had said he could not proceed with my sale, owing to a missing document concerning the right of access to the land. The mainland lawyer then told me that this sort of thing was not unheard of, and the practice disgusted him.
He asked me to tell my solicitor that there would be serious repercussions if contracts were not exchanged before the auction. He further asked me to telephone him at mid-day on the day of the auction, and if contracts had not been exchanged, then there would be an injunction put on the auction by a high court judge.
On the day of the auction, just before noon, I received a call telling me that contracts had been exchanged.

The auction was timed for 2 pm, and my son and I sat in the pub waiting to see who would be going up the stairs to the auction. Only one person arrived, and he was heard to say, "Why didn't they tell me it was called off?". I got to know this man at a later date, and realised that he was "outside of the square". He wouldn't have been told.

My Dad had had a stroke and a heart attack, and was by now semi invalid. Mum too was in poor health. We needed to provide some ground floor improvements and better facilities.

There was a small grant available, but only if the whole property was refurbished. I arranged what is now called a lifetime mortgage for my parents, which would cover the basic works. My wife and I, and our sons, all determined to contribute towards the rest of the work. We ended up re-roofing, installing double glazing and heating, re-plumbing, re-wiring, installing a new kitchen and bathroom, and completely redecorating

It was not possible to do the inside work while they were living in the property, so we arranged for them both to go into temporary care. When we visited we took photographs to show our progress. All of our sons helped with the work, which was completed the day before their golden wedding anniversary. They arrived home to a surprise party with some of their friends and even one of Mum's bridesmaids. It was a happy day, and I felt that I had given something back.

My Mums health gradually deteriorated and she died in hospital.
I so regret not saying thank you for everything.

The hardest thing I had ever done was telling my Dad that Mum had died. His health had improved slightly, and although he needed a great deal of care, his brain was still sharp, and his sense of humour wicked. My wife nursed him while it was necessary, and he died in a local nursing home having led, I'm sure, a full and fruitful life.

When the time came to manage my parents' estate, and sort out their affairs and possessions, I was expecting to find articles that appertained to my adoption. There had to be things, but I found nothing. It wouldn't surprise me at all if things hadn't been destroyed in order to keep the secret from me.

Mum and Dad had left their house to me, and I wasn't quite sure what to do with it. The mortgage had to be immediately paid off, but I wanted to do this without selling the property.
Memories were too fresh. Mum and Dad had lived in this house from the day they were married. Her grandfather had built it from scratch. It was a family house. I had been a member of this family all my known life. A decision could wait.

The property was still in good order, and required little maintenance, so eventually we decided to let it.

About this time we were burdened with a boundary dispute concerning the land purchased long ago from The Crown, which now formed part of our garden. The Land Registry and ordinance survey maps were inaccurate. They showed my neighbour's slipway hard against the wall of my workshop, when in fact it was about ten or twelve feet distant. My original deed also only showed the boundary at this wall. I maintained that the land was there when I purchased, and it had been formed into a slipway where a landing craft had been converted to a houseboat in the early 1950's. I had a sworn affidavit from the aforementioned uncle Don, who had known the area well before my time, and had been a regular visitor to the family for many years. He knew my cousin's family very well, and had worked on the local council, as had my cousin's father, the hateful and jealous uncle.

My adversary in this dispute produced affidavits sworn by both my cousins. They stated that I was incorrect, and that when I spoke of my grandfather I really was referring to their grandfather, not to mine. They also denied ever having knowledge of uncle Don.

The most damaging evidence against us was a conveyance of this parcel of land, our garden, to the plaintiff.
The plan on my conveyance was inaccurate, but we needed closure of this complete mess, and finally settled out of court, at a fraction of what the land was worth to us.

We let my parents' house for a couple of years, but I found that having had strangers occupying and re-decorating it, it no longer felt like it belonged to me. We decided to sell, and our neighbour purchased it as a buy to let.

We purchased a couple of properties which we renovated and sold on. This kept us well occupied. At home, the whole neighbourhood was changing. Large houses were being pulled down to make way for multiple, shoddily built replacements. Water frontages were being carved up to make way for ignorant, non-country-type people to act stupidly and noisily, and allow their children to shoot birds, catch crabs and pull off their legs, and generally destroy everything dear to me.

Apart from all this, I had contracted a relatively rare eye complaint, and on the day of the solar eclipse, August 11th 1999, I was told to expect total blindness, possibly within six months.
My consultant questioned me, about members of my family, as it was thought to be an hereditary disease passed through the male side. This was very worrying for us, as at the time we had three sons and three grandsons.

We considered selling up and moving to a more manageable property. If I couldn't enjoy water at the bottom of my garden, and have my boat moored there, as I had now, then I should like to have a quiet place with the sound of trees and birds, and the scent of flowers. My wife totally agreed, so we started to search for a suitable property.

We eventually found a small cottage tucked away in a nearby village. It needed a great deal of work, and the large garden was completely overgrown. We decided to go ahead, and put our own house on the market. Our boys, who were now settled in their own places, and had between them given us five wonderful grand children, were enthusiastic for us. They offered to assist with the new property, should the purchase proceed. We sold our old house and moved in September 2001, but the house wasn't habitable. We still had our boat, now in the nearby marina, and we lived aboard while the essential works to the house were carried out. I had also contracted rheumatoid arthritis and couldn't do a lot of the work. My wife and sons did enough so that we could move in just before Christmas.

Over a year had passed since my eye diagnosis, but I could still see quite well. I needed spectacles, but certainly not with a strong prescription. I was also greatly improved in my mobility, due to early diagnosis and an excellent local rheumatology clinic. We completed the cottage throughout the summer, landscaped the garden and installed a swimming pool. This was something I had been promising my wife for quite a few years.

Having completed all this, we spent most of our summer at the bottom of the garden, near the woods, in a small mobile home we had installed, overlooking a duck pond. This was a little paradise, and we decided to generate some income by letting the cottage for summer holidays, and residing in the mobile home.
Originally it had been intended for use as a changing room and somewhere for the grandchildren to stay on occasion. The cottage only had two bedrooms.

We signed up with a holiday letting company, and were fully booked the first year. Subsequently we had our own website and business was steady.

I received a telephone call one morning, claiming to be from a company of heir hunters.

I was about to dismiss this as some sort of scam and hang up, when I suddenly wondered if this could possibly be something to do with my birth family. I was asked if I was related to my Mum, and my grandmother, who they both named in full. My mind was now racing. This had to be important.

I was asked if I had been adopted. This was it, I was sure.
Had my brother found out about me and employed this firm to find me? This had to be something to do with my birth family. Everyone in my adopted family knew all about me, and most still living would likely know where I was. Anyone else would know my name, and I could be found in the telephone directory.
This, I was certain, was something to do with my birth family and my past.

Although all of this passed through my mind in a matter of seconds, and the voice on the other end of the telephone had only uttered a few words, I felt overwhelmed with hope and expectation.

I was asked if I knew my cousins, and they were named. I couldn't believe this. Could I not be left alone after all this time? I don't recall exactly what my response was, but I intimated that I wasn't interested any further, and made to disconnect.

The person on the line spoke quite sharply to me, explaining that this was all to do with a small inheritance from one of my Mum's nieces, and gave her name. He enquired as to whether I knew her father's name and his relationship with my grandmother.

This now sounded genuine, and I asked for further details.
Why was he asking if he already knew who I was, and had obtained my telephone number.

Apparently Mum's niece had died intestate and this company were seeking heirs to her estate. This was the singing daughter of Mum's uncle, known as "Putty"

My Mum and her sister had been easy to trace, and as both were deceased, then the children were next in line. My cousins were easily found, but they had stated that they had no knowledge of my Mum having a child!.

Apparently though, further enquiries were made and it was established that I had been adopted into the family. I was therefore an heir to the estate. I was told that I would be contacted again.

Some weeks later I received a cheque, and a list of beneficiaries.
I admit to a little satisfaction that the amount I received was the same sum as that shared by my cousins.

No knowledge of me indeed!

My eyes deteriorated slightly, and often made me think about my birth parents. It was now thought by my specialist that the complaint was passed through the female side. So, which of my birth parents might have suffered, and did they actually go blind? I wanted to know.
My wife was still hesitant about trying to find out anything about my birth family, but I kept thinking of that brother who might be out there somewhere. Was he blind?
I didn't expect that my Mother would still be alive, but I didn't know how old she might be. She was married, that I had been told, so she wouldn't have been a teenage mum in 1940, surely? She would probably be in her late eighties were she still alive.
Time was marching on, and my brother would be approaching his three score years and ten. I couldn't leave it any longer. I had to try. I had heard that the Salvation Army and Dr Barnardo's were known to be involved in adoptions, and decided to give them both a call.

Neither the Salvation Army nor Dr Barnardo's could help me, so I tried the Red Cross, I knew they were prominent in London during the war, and I had come from there. I was hopeful. I remembered that my Mum had been in this organisation and had attended a garden party at Buckingham Palace in recognition of her work in the local hospital. My wife, when chairperson of the local Parish Council, had also been to a Buckingham Palace garden party, and I had accompanied her there. This, I thought, was a good omen.

Unfortunately my hopes were dashed. They couldn't help me either. Somehow, I was now thinking straight. This was all to do with my Mum. Where were the clues? She had left me nothing by way of a paper clue, but there was one there somewhere. There had to be.

I remembered my Mum collecting annually for the National Children's Home. I found their number, and dialled. My heart was in my mouth when they answered the telephone. I was asked what my birth name was. "I didn't have any other name", I told them. "I've always had this one".

"Very well", was the reply. "Then can you tell me your adoptive parents' names, and their address at the time you were adopted?". Of course I could. They never had any other address, and I gave them the details.

The next statement amazed me. The lady said, "Yes John, you are one of our children, and we still have your complete file. Would you like me to make an appointment for you to see it?"

I couldn't believe this was happening. After sixty four years I was going to find out who I really was. It scared me.

A week or so later I received a letter inviting me to Horsham, their nearest office to me, during the following week.

I hadn't told my wife or our boys anything about this, although I thought I should have. The night before my appointment, out of the blue, my wife said "What about searching for your past now we are settled?" "I shall know all about it tomorrow", I told her, and asked if she would like to accompany me. We were excited, if a bit apprehensive.

We arrived at Horsham in good time to keep my appointment, and I was feeling very nervous. I knew absolutely nothing about from where or from whom I had come, but now I was about to find out. Had I been told the truth when aged nine?
Were my parents dead at that time? Was Auntie Margaret my mother, and was my father tortured by the Japanese?
Questions. Questions that might be answered very soon.
What would be in my file?

Well Worth Waiting For

Would my file even contain the information I now desperately needed to know, or would it only relate to my Mum and Dad adopting a baby from a Home? There may not be any information further back than that.

Ten minutes to go. A coffee from the flask, and a deep drag on my pipe, and I was ready for whatever might come. At least I thought so.....

We were met by Margaret Phelps. a charming lady who asked us to sit so that she could give some background information before opening the file. I could see the file on her desk. It was quite a thick folder, and I judged that it would be quite extensive. Not just from when I was collected . . . .

THE

NATIONAL CHILDRENS HOME

Highbury Park, London .N.5.

Appn No. 36375   Date 19-5-42.

APPLICATION for the Admission of,

Hayler   Harold

Long Eaton   Age 3 months

Before Principal 19-5-42.

RESULT ....   Admit

Payment.....................

Admitted to ...   Akrill House, Harpenden. 15-7-42.

Revision.....

Transferred to......

Re-ADMITTED...

LEFT THE HOME   Adopted 20th August '1942.

The cover of my National Children's Home file.

The first statement made was that she thought I should like to know my original name, my birth name. I had already told the person I originally spoke to, in my initial telephone call, that I had only ever had one name, the one I had now. I was so young. Why should I have ever had any other name?

The lady smiled and said, "Your Mother named you Harold".

She then said, "Harold Hayler, after her own surname".

So, if she was married, then her husband was my father after all. His name would be Hayler too.

"Not so" I was told. "Your Fathers name was Gammon, Fredrick Gammon. He and your Mother were not married".

"Bastard", my uncle had called me, so that bit was right after all, but it mattered nothing to me. My Mother called me Harold.
A good old English name!

At least it wasn't Dai, or Dafydd, or something Welsh.

When my file was opened, and each page briefly referred to, I became confused. It was all too much to take in. There was little information about my Father, other than a good character reference from my Mother, whose name was Audrey. There was also a scathing opinion of him from her brother Raymond.

According to Audrey, my Father's widowed mother, lived in Wales at the time of my birth. She would be my grandmother. Probably, then, my Father was a Welshman!!!.

It suddenly came back to me. My Dad had said "I never did like bloody Welshmen". Little did I know he meant me, or at least my Father. The truth was coming out at last.

I saw my Mum's handwriting, letters longing for a child. I also saw my Mother Audrey's handwriting, having to give one up. I saw the almost desperate letters of my Mother's brother, Raymond, on her behalf. It was all too much.

All this had been going on in the middle of a war, and these people were beside themselves with worry because of me. Not that I was responsible, but if it wasn't for me, then these people might have been happy. My brother had been taken away from our Mother because of me. What would he think about me if he knew the reason?

I had to excuse myself for a few minutes and compose myself.

My Mum and Dad who brought me up were dead, but what about my Mother, my Father, my brother, or even uncle Raymond. Would they still be alive, and would they want to know me if ever they could be found?.

I was recommended to an organisation which might help to trace my family, or families. I understood that any approach would have to be handled very delicately. It was not something I felt that I could do myself.

We returned to the Island to await my file which would, I was assured, contain mostly original letters and forms.

I here enclose my notes from what I could remember of the very emotional day, when I found out after sixty four years, who I really was.

I made notes on my return from my meeting at NCH Horsham, as far as I could remember, while I awaited my file.

John Sheen

I was born in Derbyshire, England.

Birth date April 11th 1942, Named Harold, with my mother's surname of Hayler. Her name was Audrey, possibly Audrey Helen. She was a married woman aged twenty eight. Maiden name probably Ashmore.
I stayed with my mother for two months.

My father's name was Frederick Roger Gammon.
He was a soldier. His widowed mother lived in Wales.
He was not married to my mother. It is not known if he was married. He was a painter and decorator by trade.

I had a brother 3yrs old, who was taken away from our mother by his fathers family. I don't know his name.

Before I was able to be accepted at the Home, I was sent to a foster home where my Ration Book went missing.

My placing at the National Children's Home was arranged by my mother's brother Mr Raymond Ashmore. My mother, with the help of her brother paid 5/—per week towards my keep at the Home, and for a month after my adoption, apparently in case I was returned to her before being legally adopted.

I was 4 months old when I was handed over, by the engine of the Portsmouth train, at Waterloo Station by a woman wearing a brown hat and a fawn coat.

There are letters in my file between the Home and Raymond Ashmore, and my Mum and the Home.
There is one letter written by Audrey my mother. I have touched something that she had touched.

My mother's husband was a prisoner of war, and was going to divorce her. He insisted that I be disposed of, then he would forgive and forget.

It is not clear what my father's position was, but according to letters he was in no position to do anything.

I have searched what records I can find, and I believe that my mother was born 19th June 1913.
She died in November 1997. Registered near her address in 1942.

A similar search indicates that my father, Frederick Roger Gammon was born 24th February 1913.
He died in August 1984 Registered Radnorshire Powys, Wales.

It is distressing that my first discoveries are the Death Records of both of my biological parents. I would have liked to thank them for my life. Indications are that their affair was serious.
My mother spoke highly of my father, and had his home address and army details. They will never know how sorry I am for not trying to find them before it was too late.

I intend to try to find my half brother before it is too late. He knew our mother, and could tell me about her. He might have her photograph.

Any inaccuracies in these notes will be evident when I receive my file.

John Sheen

My file arrived about a week after my meeting at National Children's Home. It seemed bigger than I had remembered.

I could now take my time and read every word. There had not been time at my meeting. I had tried to remember as much as I could when writing my initial notes, which I have included within this narrative, but there was so much more detail to be discovered.

I was born in Derbyshire at the Nightingale Home, three days early. Audrey Hayler, my Mother, was a married woman with a three year old son. Her husband was a prisoner of war, but quite where is not clear. There is no mention of anything Japanese.

My Father had been on active service in Derby, manning a gun emplacement there. His name was Frederick Roger Gammon, and he was a painter and decorator by trade.

My putting up for adoption was applied for by my Mother's brother Raymond Ashmore, who lived in Sheffield. He had a poor opinion of my Father, and of my Mother too, so it appeared, although he worked hard for her under the "very distressing circumstances" in which his sister found herself.
He spent the princely sum of eight pounds with a solicitor, trying to get my Father convicted. Of what I'm not sure.
He seems to have had no help from my Mother in his quest against my Father, for she spoke highly of him. She wrote that he was romantic, kind, and had been very helpful to local people. She also said that he had a winning way with him. Perhaps that was lucky for me. I might not have been here otherwise. It seems to have been a meaningful affair of some standing.

I started with Ancestry.co.uk, and searched for Audrey Hayler. It was the most harrowing experience to see her name, including her middle name of Helen, appear in front of me in print, telling me that she had died in 1997. She had still been living in her home town. I was truly gutted, angry and distraught to think that I had wasted all those years, when I might have, could have, in fact found her.

It would be difficult for anyone to understand how someone, never met or known, could be so missed, but I missed my real Mother equally as much as I missed my adoptive parents, with whom I had spent all of my life. I was overcome with emotion, and I cried and sobbed like the baby I was when she last saw me. Just to see her name now makes me feel wretched. I feel ashamed, and that I let her down badly.

I realise of course that it's entirely possible that my Mother may not have wanted any contact with me. I believe this often happens when adoptees find their birth parents, but I could understand and accept that. I just wanted to tell her that I understood how things were for her, and that I could never blame her for giving me up. I should have liked to hold her hand for a moment, touch her hair, and see the colour of her eyes. Most of all I would have liked to tell her that I loved her, and say "Thank you for my life Mum. It's been a good one, and I have been happy".

In my file there is a handwritten letter which she sent to the National Children's Home. The letter was not for me, and it doesn't even mention me, but it shows that she had beautiful handwriting, full of poise and flowing beauty. I'm sure she must have been like that too.
I have the letter now, and I shall always treasure it. It is the one thing I have that we have both touched, albeit many years apart.
I hope someday that I can find her picture so that I can perhaps see what attracted my Father, and encouraged him to exercise his romantic and winning ways with her.

When I discovered that my Father Frederick Roger Gammon had died in Knighton, and the death was registered in Radnorshire, Powys, it was obvious that he had returned to the town in which he was born.

I contacted the Registry Office concerned, only to find it was at a solicitor's office in Station Road, Knighton. The registrar was very interested in my story, and told me that there were still members of a Gammon family living in and around the town.
He suggested that I might visit Knighton at some time, and either he or his wife, who he said was "keen on this sort of thing", would go through the whole register with me, and possibly find family members still alive. In any case it would be an opportunity to glean information for a family tree.

I determined that one day I would take him up on his suggestion.
In the mean time he would send me a copy my Father's death certificate

I knew that my Father was in the army during the war. His rank and service number were included in one of the letters written by Raymond Ashmore. I presume my Mother had furnished this information. His home address in Harrow was also given, and I wondered if she had corresponded with him whilst he was on duty and at home. It seemed more than likely. It was now quite clear that my parents had eventually gone their separate ways. I hoped my Mother had her son returned to her.

Armed with my Father's army number I contacted the records office and applied for a copy of his service record.
I wasn't especially interested in his service, but I wanted to know how close to Long Eaton he was stationed, and whether it had been easy for him to visit my Mother. She had stated that he had been very helpful to local people, so I guessed where he must have spent his leave time.

I now knew that my Mother had died in her own home town of Long Eaton, the town I had come from. I wanted to go there, and possibly to Wales. We rented a cottage in the Derbyshire Dales, at a place called Two Dales, and made a provisional booking at a farm cottage in Knighton for the following week.

On the first morning in Derbyshire we drove to Long Eaton, and further on, into Old Sawley. We stopped for lunch at the Nag's Head, which was very quiet for the time of day. We got into conversation with the landlord and the barmaid, whose uncle, it turned out, runs a coach company on our Island. I asked if I might borrow their telephone directory, hoping that I might find a listing for Hayler. There were none.

As conversation progressed, the reason for our visit unfurled, and amazingly Gavin the landlord told us that there was a Mr Hayler living just nearby. Apparently the old gentleman used to be a regular at the pub, but was now somewhat infirm. He suggested we pay Mr Hayler a visit.

Deciding not to waste such an opportunity, and yet being very cautious of what I might enquire, we knocked on the door of a small bungalow.

Fortunately the door was opened by a lady who said she was a home help. I told her that I was trying to trace the Hayler family of Long Eaton, and that the pub landlord had suggested this visit. She assured us that Mr Hayler would welcome a visit, and invited us in. The gentleman rolled off about a dozen names of his relations from around the world, but had never heard of Audrey Hayler. We spent a pleasant hour or so, and listened with interest to this man relating his family memories. There was nothing there that led me towards my own family.

Driving back to Long Eaton, I decided to at least find something associated with my Mother. I had her address at the time of my birth, and decided to see if I could find where she had lived.
I had been with my Mother, I knew, for at least two months, before I went to a foster home, prior to being accepted by the National Children's Home. If I was not going to find my family, then I could perhaps find some place where they, and I, had once been.

Dove Lane was found to be a small cul-de-sac off of the busy Derby Road. It is a leafy and quiet lane with residential buildings at the end. We parked and walked to the end where we saw a waste bin with a large number four painted on it. This, then, was my Mother's home during the war, and possibly afterwards, depending on whether or not her husband had returned, and not divorced her. While I stood just looking at the house and wondering if my Father had ever gone through the front door, or made a stealthy approach from the rear, a woman dressed in a nurse's uniform approached from the neighbouring house, and asked if she could be of assistance.

I explained that my Mother had lived at number four many years ago, and that I was just curious to see the place. The lady said that the occupants would be very interested to know about my mother, and proceeded to go through the gate and knock on the door. An elderly lady answered the door, and my interest was explained to her, by her, obviously close, neighbour. We were immediately asked to come in to the house, and the lady and her husband introduced themselves. They had lived here for many years.

Once again I found myself full of emotion. I had been here before. I must have been fed and changed and bathed here. We were shown things about the house that our hosts thought would not have been changed at all since my Mother was there, and also told of alterations they had made. We were asked to stay for tea and cake. It was a wonderful experience.

Before we left I had my photograph taken by the front door of number four Dove Lane. I was happy that I had returned.

We ate an early evening meal at Eaton Farm, a fairly modern pub type restaurant, before returning to Two Dales. Not a particularly productive day, but I had found one Hayler, so they did exist, even if not my Haylers.

I had with me the printout I had taken from the internet of my Mother's death registration at Ilkeston, and the telephone number of the registry office. I telephoned the following morning and enquired about a copy death certificate for Audrey Hayler, and gave an approximate date of death. It was arranged that I could collect a copy certificate later that day. I held the certificate in my hand, with that empty feeling I had felt when first I saw that my Mother had died.

What I didn't notice, at first, was that the death had been registered by Audrey's daughter. This was beyond belief. A sister! I would not have been surprised if Audrey's son, my brother, had been named on the certificate, because I knew he existed, or rather he did in 1942, but a sister! I hadn't expected that. Her address at the time was also stated, but there was no way I intended to approach in that direction.

The name on the certificate was, to me, at least, unusual. I guessed then that this lady would be married. She wasn't a Miss Hayler any longer. This was good news indeed. I could now search two different names, which I hoped would lead to my family.

The next stop was a Wimpy Bar and a loan of yet another telephone directory. All the public boxes were empty.
There was just one listing of the name I was looking for, and I transferred the number to my mobile. I now didn't know quite what to do. I hesitated to make any approach, as there was only the one single name to go on.

On our return to the cottage I rehearsed what I might say if my call was answered, and punched in the numbers.

My call was answered by a female voice, sounding quite young.
It was doubtful this could be Audrey's daughter, but perhaps a granddaughter. I apologised for the intrusion and explained that I was in the process of constructing a family tree, and that I understood someone of her name may be related to the Hayler family. She said that she was not, but she knew someone that was. I asked if I might relay my telephone number through her, and she agreed.

About twenty minutes later my telephone rang, and another lady enquired as to who I was, and what was my interest in the Hayler family. I explained, as before, that I was researching my family tree, and gave my name. I was told quite emphatically that her family tree had been researched and documented, and I was certainly not on it. I hadn't expected that I would be. The lady wanted to know how I had obtained her name, and how I had connected her with the name Hayler.

I said that I had that day obtained the death certificate of Audrey Hayler, and I knew that the death had been registered by her daughter. She told me that Audrey Hayler was her mother.

I clammed up. This was my sister I was talking to. I could hardly speak. This wasn't working out as I had hoped or planned. I shouldn't have got myself into this position. Having established a connection, I intended for the National Children's Home to make enquiries and a discreet approach. I was now being pressed for answers. I couldn't see it through.

I was shaking. "Please will you talk to my wife?" I asked, but the response was that there was no point in that. I gave the phone to my wife anyway. She related the basic facts about my adoption and answered a few leading questions, including one quite obscure one. Where had Raymond Ashmore lived in 1942? The address was in my file and was read out from one of his letters. Upon getting the answer, this lady who I was now certain was my sister, took a short breath and asked if I was still there. My wife was asked to tell me that I had two sisters and a brother, and was asked when we could meet. Sunday lunch was agreed at the Eaton Farm, where we had dined the previous day.

I was unable to speak further to this, the first member of my birth family who I had now found. I was completely overcome with emotion, elated, excited and at the same time fearful. I could not believe that within the last five minutes or so, for it was no longer than that, I had been talking to a member of the family to which I had originally belonged, even if it was for only a short time, and sixty four years past.

But there were doubts. Would I be accepted, or would the arranged meeting be just out of curiosity? Had my wife really been believed when she had given the information that she had?
It had all happened so quickly. I was now aware of two sisters and a brother. Was this brother my Mother's son, who had been taken away from her because of me? I would soon know.

What I couldn't understand was the immediate desire of my sister, for she had confirmed that she was my sister, to meet me.
I was now beginning to think that this family had perhaps been expecting me to turn up one day. The fact that I had been kept in ignorance of my adoption, may not have been reciprocated within my birth family. It was entirely possible that having been adopted away, I had been forgotten about, and thought of as being someone else's child. My Mum had convinced

herself that she had given birth to me. Perhaps the Hayler family saw it in a similar way. I didn't belong in their family. I went to another family.

To be accepted, or at least to be offered a face to face meeting without there being any previous knowledge of me, seemed unlikely.

It was different for me. I was desperate to find these people whose family members, alive in the 1940's I knew about. I had letters they had written, but would this Hayler family be so openly welcoming if they didn't have at least some knowledge of me. I somehow doubted it. Perhaps I was expected to turn up one day, and the questions asked of me and of my wife were to check that it was me, the illegitimate child of Audrey Hayler.

The next day was a Saturday, and we had promised to drive over to Southport in Lancashire to visit my uncle Don's third wife, her daughter and son-in-law.
His previous wife, the girls and young Paul's mother, had died some years previously. Don and his new wife Ethel had been regular visitors to us on the Island, until he had passed away.

When uncle Don died, we scattered his ashes on the river from our motor cruiser. It was his wish to be returned to the place on the Island that he loved. Ethel and her grand daughter accompanied us. Ethel had returned a couple of times since with her daughter and son-in-law, and spent days with us.

On one of these occasions we were sitting in the garden talking, and the subject of medicine came up. I was at that time partaking in a trial of a new anti-inflammatory drug. I happened to mention the name of the doctor whose care I was under, and it transpired that he and our guest had arrived in this country together to commence training. Neither had returned home after qualifying. My doctor was a primarily a diabetes consultant, and our guest was a well respected gynaecologist.

When they arrived in this country in the 1960's they were mystified by thousands of screaming girls at the airport. Upon enquiring what was happening, they were told that the beetles were coming.
They thought that this must be something terrible to cause such hysterical behaviour. A storm of locusts would be bad enough, but beetles? They

were anxious. Further enquiries revealed that the next flight to land was carrying "The Beatles".

I phoned my doctor and connected him with someone he hadn't been in contact with for over forty years. Both men were pleased at what this coincidence had brought.

Uncle Don once told a story about our guest the gynaecologist. He had asked him if, by virtue of his job, did he ever lose interest in sex. The reply was, "Does a banker ever lose interest in money?"

We spent an enjoyable day at Southport, remembering old times. It was a welcome break from the many emotions of my family search.

I awoke on Sunday morning excited, if a little apprehensive.
Today was one of the biggest in my life.
My sister had said that she was probably recognisable by her size, and that her disabled husband would be with her.
She said that our brother would most likely not attend, as he lived in South Devon. Our other sister, Barbara, had married and emigrated to Australia when she was a very young woman.

We arrived at Eaton Farm, parked the car, and made our way inside. Coming towards us was a, not really, very large woman, dressed in a pale green trouser suit, and her arms were outstretched towards me, She reminded me of a green galleon in full sail.

We hugged, both with tears in our eyes, and our respective partners were introduced.

As we made our way through the bar, I noticed a man standing in the bay window. He somehow looked familiar to me. The resemblance to me was most noticeable. We could have passed for brothers. He was just like I'd expected a brother to look when I had often taken notice of boys, then men, just in case.
"Hello brother", he said., and we shook hands. He had driven up from Devon to meet us.

Well Worth Waiting For

Obviously there was no doubt that I belonged with these people.
The chemistry between us was measurable. I had brought with me no evidence of who I was, other than that I had kept an appointment made on the telephone two days ago. I needed nothing else. This was a meeting of family members. It was very humbling for me. I had appeared from nowhere, and yet I felt that I belonged here. Already. I was accepted.

Nobody in the entire Hayler family had any knowledge of me until two days ago, save for a very elderly aunt of my brother and sister's. She had overheard an argument between Audrey's husbands sisters when very young. It was something to do with Audrey and a baby.
This had been reported in response to my sister passing the news of my existence, over the weekend

We enjoyed a champagne lunch, with much talk of Audrey, and also of my life as an adoptee. I wished my Mum and Dad could have been there, and heard it said, that I probably had a happier childhood where I was, than if I had not been adopted. I should also have liked them to know that I wouldn't compare them, and that I would never forget what they had done for me. I was sorry that this meeting didn't happen long before, but what was here now, was well worth waiting for.

With my brother and sister. November 12th, 2006.

We all retired to my sister and brother-in-laws bungalow and I produced my file. There was so much information that I found it best to answer the many questions about Audrey, and Uncle Raymond, by producing their letters. It was a revelation to my new brother and sister.

Not one word had ever been uttered about me in the whole of my brother and sister's lives. They must have been shocked by what had transpired. We were told about their father, Audrey's husband, and learnt that he was a prisoner in Italy, not in a Japanese camp, and that there had been three telegrams concerning his capture and also his being missing.

Maybe Audrey hadn't expected her husband ever to return, and she and Fred had made plans that had to be aborted when her husband was confirmed alive. Something we shall never know.

My sister Christine produced a photo album, and at last I saw photographs of my mother. I already knew that she would look beautiful. There were many family pictures, and I was introduced in this way to my grand parents and other relations, including Uncle Raymond Ashmore. I forgave him for comparing my Father to Hitler, and his hope that they would both end up the same way. Well they were both painters and decorators.

My Mother with Sid. Happy to get him back.

Christine was our hostess and, quite rightly, led the majority of the conversation, and gave the information that I badly wanted to know. Sid, our brother, had to leave in order to drive back to Devon, but promised to visit us on the Island in the near future.

Bob, my new brother-in-law, entertained my wife with various background information concerning his life, and the latter years of Audrey's life, when he and Christine kept a close eye on her.

Every so often Christine and I were in tears over some fact or other that meant something to us both. She relating memories of our Mother, and me, trying to understand how it might have been for her. I was pleased that she seemed to think no less of Audrey because of me, and her affair with Fred.

I was overwhelmed by the bond that had already developed between us. Strangers hours before, now as close as if we had grown up together, and never been apart. It was also as though we had missed each other, and had to make up for time lost.

Audrey had worked very hard during her life. She was a splendid cook, and a devoted mother to her children.
I somehow felt included. I had been with my Mother for the first two months of my life.

She was employed for a long time in school meals, and on her retirement was presented with a handsome clock, complete with a brass plate showing appreciation for what she had done.
Christine presented me with this clock. The second thing both my Mother and I had touched, but many years apart.
I felt honoured to be given it, as well as some silver spoons that had belonged to our grandmother.

It was hard to leave that day, because I really felt that I had come home at last.

Grandma and Grandad Ashmore. My Mother's parents.

We quite reluctantly said goodbye to Long Eaton on the Monday morning, and headed for Derby, prior to setting off for Wales. I wanted to see if the Nightingale Maternity Home was still there.

We got our directions from a police car parked on a busy road. The officer didn't question that my wife was obviously not in need of such a place, and I suppose I looked too old to be an expectant father, so we didn't get offered an escort.

We eventually found the Nightingale Home, a fine red brick building with an over-door niche. There is a life size statue of Florence Nightingale within the niche, holding her lamp. I went up the steps and had my photograph taken there. The maternity home was originally situated at the rear of this building, and the site was now due to be re-developed.

I was not very impressed with what little I saw of the city itself. It was very busy, very grey, and there were too many people. Not what I was used to.

The Dales, and all the countryside that we had seen, was wonderful. The trees were turning into their autumn colours, and it was like our Island, but on a massive scale. It is said that there is a little bit of every part of England, in miniature, on the Island, but there are very few areas that are busy, and grey, and parts are only crowded in the summer holidays. I knew I would come back to The Dales, and to Long Eaton. I have family there.

The Nightingale Home.

It was a pleasant drive to Wales, and when I saw the first sign spelling out Knighton, I wondered what I would find there. We drove into town and parked in the car park at the rear of the hotel. Walking through the archway into Broad street gave me an amazing feeling. I looked up the street to the clock tower, and I honestly felt that I was home. Everything around me seemed familiar. It's not a busy town, and quite small as town centres go, but I felt that home coming feeling that I had when meeting my brother and sister. This time though it was the place itself. I knew my father was born and died there, but I also knew from my file letters and the address Audrey had given to Uncle Raymond, that he had probably lived mostly in England. I felt he was here now, waiting for me. My wife remarked that she had a strange, but pleasant feeling for the place, and that accurately described how I felt too.

We went across towards the Horse and Jockey to get a late lunch, and noticed a young man up a ladder, painting a building. My wife and I looked at each other startled. The man on the ladder was the image of myself at his age. He had lots of curly hair, and wore a white boiler-suit, as I usually had done at work. Something weird was happening here, and there was no explanation for it.

I had never heard of Knighton, Wales, before my file informed that my Father's widowed mother lived there. We have a village called Knighton on the Island, but I hadn't ever heard of another. I felt that I was being drawn into this place, not against my will, but being helped along somehow. It was very strange.

We joked that the house painter might be a Gammon, a grandson of Fred perhaps. There was no doubt that my brother Sid and I were alike now, in mature years, but according to the photographs we had seen, we differed greatly in our younger days.

After our meal we sought out our cottage in Woodhouse Lane, and settled in. I then phoned the Registrar and made an appointment for the following afternoon.
I couldn't wait to go back out and explore. I had the address of Fred's Knighton home, and I asked someone for directions. It was beyond walking distance, so we drove just out of the town to find it. It was a fairly modern house on a small estate. The current occupants have children, judging by the toys in the front garden.

The next port of call was Brookside, the place where Fred was born. It is a quaint row of cottages, by a brook of course, and in the town. We had missed this place earlier, which could plainly be seen from the main street where we saw the decorator. I don't believe in ghosts, but I was feeling that something was going on which I didn't understand . . . . nothing sinister . . . . it was rather comforting actually. Like a pleasant dream that couldn't quite be remembered. The ladder man was nowhere to be seen by now.

We walked back up the town past the clock tower and into narrow streets lined with ancient buildings. Some little old shops were still trading, but others were either boarded up or converted. This must have been a thriving town once upon a time. Some of it was now dying. I should like to have been here when my Father was a boy. I would have found it magical. I did now.

We needed to refuel the car, and called at the nearby petrol station. To the rear of this was a supermarket, low and rambling, selling everything you could think of. It is little wonder that we had found boarded up little shops, which at one time were part of the heart and soul of this lovely little old market town.

We found the Offa's Dyke Centre and collected a brochure. This is about midway along the Dyke, the earthworks constructed in the eighth century on the orders of Offa, King of Mercia. It roughly follows the border between England and Wales. The Welsh name for Knighton is Tref-y-Clawdd, the town on the Dyke, and actually part of the town is in England.

From the centre there is access to the River Teme, and we walked along the bank for some distance before returning to keep our appointment. We had taken our dog Leo with us, and he ran through the river, which is very shallow around this location, as much as he did on the wooded banks.

We found the solicitor's office in Station Road, a large, rather unkempt property. It looked almost deserted.
We were shown into an office which could have been in a Dickens novel. Files and boxes everywhere. There were several registers on the desk, with various coloured tabs protruding from them. It was obvious that some provisional work had been carried out on my behalf.

The Registrar gave us a brief history of the Gammon family as portrayed in the records he held. This was very interesting, but too involved to be taken in immediately. He had already prepared a list of those family members whose deaths hadn't yet been registered, so that I might try to trace those still living. I was so grateful for this, as I could have spent many hours searching myself. He said "I think I know your uncle, Walter Gammon". He then checked his notes and corrected himself. "No", he said, "this chap is your cousin. Fred Gammon was his uncle. Wally lives in Knighton, you should go and see him". I explained that I had already made a mistake, or so I thought, in approaching my Mother's family the way I did, and I wasn't about to do it again.

Finding my family at Long Eaton had been an unbelievable experience. Not what I had remotely expected, or intended.
I was the one with the information, the Haylers, as it turned out, knew nothing, although I hadn't known that. The experience could not have been more wonderful than it was. I was not prepared to chance anything with the Gammons, my Father's family. This was going to be completely different. They might or might not know of my existence, and if they did, the response might be hostile There was no way of knowing.

Fred's children may well live in this town, and I wasn't about to turn up out of the blue. I now had Mr Wally Gammon's address and the National Children's Home would make enquiries for me.
I was pleased to learn about my Father's family, but there was no question of my approaching any member of it myself.

The Registrar passed me Mr Gammon's phone number and again, saying that he knew him, suggested that it was a pity to waste the opportunity of being this close and that I should take it. "What is there to lose? He will either say "Come and see me", or tell you to bugger off. At least you will know where you stand and can progress from there". I told him I'd think about it. It didn't take long.

Well Worth Waiting For

The Clock Tower. Broad Street, Knighton.

There was no network connection in the town, so I went to the public box beneath the Clock Tower, and dialled.
The "Hello" sounded friendly. "Is that Mr Wally Gammon?" I asked.
"Hello Bill" he said. "Ah Um, actually I'm not Bill. My name is John".
"I'm sorry," he said, "I thought you were my cousin". "Well, actually Mr Gammon, I've got news for you. I am your cousin".
"How do you make that out?" he replied.
"Did you have an uncle Fred?" I asked.
"Yes, we did. "Curly" we called him".
My thoughts went to the man on the ladder.

I explained that I was born during the war when his uncle Fred was in the army, and that he was my Father. Mr Gammon laughed. He asked where I was now, and I told him. "Come round and see me" he said, and confirmed the address that I had for him. We arranged to call at six o'clock that evening.

We pulled up outside of a nice looking bungalow and got out of the car. The front door opened, and a man stood in the light of the porch, smiling. "Come on in cousin" he invited.
I couldn't believe it. I thought the Registrar must have called him after we left the office. On the other hand, his laugh, when I had said about being the wartime son of Fred, perhaps struck a chord.

I liked this man immediately. His son Mike, was waiting in the lounge and we exchanged pleasantries. I explained to them both about myself, and how I had arrived at this point in my search. I had brought with me my file, so as to confirm what I was telling them. I had my birth certificate, but the space for my Father's name was blank. That wasn't evidence. Uncle Raymond's letters about Fred were the best that I had. They were not really necessary.

These two men who I had met only a few minutes ago, were talking to me as though I was uncle Fred's son. I knew that I was, of course, but they had no idea before my afternoon phone call. The Registrar had not phoned to warn this man, my first Welsh cousin, sitting here now with my second cousin. I was astounded. I felt once again accepted on face value.

We heard about the relations living in the town and nearby, and those scattered throughout the whole of the British Isles. We also learned that Fred had a daughter, a little younger than me. Fred had returned to Knighton when he retired, with his second wife, who was not the mother of the child. So, I had another sister somewhere. She did not live in Knighton.

The information that was given by both these men was too much to take in all at once. Wally said that he had phoned his sister Jean, who lived in the town, to tell her about my call to him. She was concerned, and suggested that I might be some trickster trying to steal his television or clock. After a while the telephone rang. It was Jean, to enquire whether I had turned up. Wally told her that I had, and asked if she would like to speak with me. He handed me the phone.
"Hello Jean, would you like to buy a cheap television or a clock?"
Her response was, "That's Fred alright".

Before we left our new cousins we agreed to meet again tomorrow. Jean had invited us to her home for coffee. It was likely that Doreen, the widow of Wally's twin brother Bill, would also be there. Further up the town lived Phyllis, known as Auntie Dill, and her husband, and Barbara, their daughter. I was told that Dill might not be much interested. She had lost her sight in her later years. Apparently she had idolised Fred all her life, and didn't get on with the wife he had brought back to the town when he retired. As nothing was known about me, or who my Mother was, this might not meet Dill's approval. I could certainly understand such a scenario.

We called at Wally's in the morning in order to be taken to this family meeting. Looking out of Wally's window the view was lovely, There were rolling hills covered in trees, a forest in fact. Seeing us looking, Wally said,
"Can you see the eee errr?"
"Eee err?" I exclaimed.
"No, no, eeee errrr", he said.
Now there is only a mild Welsh flavour to his accent, but we didn't get it. On the distant forest slope were the letters "E. R" planted in contrasting colour trees. It was quite plain now, when pointed out. It had been done to commemorate the Queen's Coronation in 1953.

Arriving at Jean's, we were led straight in, no knocking, straight through the kitchen, and into the sitting room. Three ladies stood talking. Wally introduced them. Jean was a very happy looking lady, who looked busy even standing still. Cousin Barbara, a second cousin, told me straight away that Fred was her favourite uncle. Doreen, an elegant, smart looking lady, seemed almost shy on introduction.

An elderly lady, wearing opaque spectacles, sat in an arm chair, and Barbara introduced us to her mother. The lady stretched out her hand towards me and said, "Fred, Fred". I took her hand and knelt beside her. "I loved Fred", she said, and held me tighter. "Fred, my favourite", she said. "We had such fun together". Her navy blue skirt was getting damp now. We were both crying. "I'll tell you all about my Fred", she said. This was my auntie Dill, who loved my Father as I knew I could love her.

John Sheen

Jean, Doreen, Self, Auntie Dill, Barbara and Wally.

Barbara had to leave for work, and Auntie Dill was taken home. I promised to come and see her soon. Those of us left enjoyed a lunch, together with Jean's son John. He had plenty to tell me about his great uncle Fred, as did the others. I was in a state of utter disbelief that these people had all accepted us both in the way that they had. Long Eaton was beyond belief, and now it was happening again, here on the other side of my newly found families. I was so fortunate to have been born of such genuine, caring and loving people. My Mum and Dad who brought me up were the same. Some strange ideas perhaps, but they had done their best for me. Fortunate? Lucky? I didn't know the words to describe how I felt about it, but I was, and am, thankful to everyone.

I was given the addresses and numbers of all the other cousins according to Jean's address book. There were fourteen of them, plus their children. I learnt that Fred was one of nine children, and was told many facts and stories about the whole family. I could not have known more if I had been one of them for years. It was so interesting hearing each of them voicing their own personal memories.

I learnt that Fred had run away with a visiting circus when he was young, and jumped off of the Knucklas Viaduct holding an umbrella as a parachute. He broke his collar bone. There were many stories being told, which I hoped would be repeated at a later time, as I was still full of emotion and couldn't grasp it all.

On the Saturday night everyone who could make it came to The Horse and Jockey for a celebratory meal. Twice within a week I was in the midst of my birth families. It had all happened so quickly. It was not just because I had been lucky with my search, but because of the people I had found in two separate places, who were unknown to each other.

I would argue with my Dad about "Bloody Welshmen" now, but if he was here he would know that those I had met were special people indeed. My Mum, had she been at Long Eaton would have understood, and I'm certain be pleased that I had found out about my birth Mother. She would realise that she had nothing to fear by telling me the truth.

On the day of departure from Wales, Wally gave me the photograph album that was a retirement gift to Fred from Kodak, where he had worked. It had been filled with photographs of the family, from the earliest days. There was my great-grandmother sitting amongst her eight children, Auntie Dill the youngest. There was a photograph of great-granddad Samuel as well. He had also copied various birth and death certificates, and Mike, his son, had supplied a printout of the Gammon family tree which he had researched. I wasn't on it. Not yet, anyway . . . .

The Gammon family. Walter, Margery, Joe, Nelly, Fred, Val. Mary, Granny, Phyllis.

Grandad. Samuel Charles Gammon.

There was one particular photograph of Fred with his brothers. It was almost like I was looking in a mirror when I was in my early twenties. We were so similar. Again I thought of the man on the ladder. The three of us had the same curly hair.

Jean presented me with the gold tie-pin that my Father had given her years before, and Barbara had prepared a selection of photographs of Fred in various guises, and at various ages too. There wasn't one of when he dressed up as a tramp and pretended to beg. Apparently people in the town couldn't recognise him.

There were also photographs of Fred's daughter, my sister, both on her own and with him. She was truly a beautiful little girl. He had called her his little princess. You could see why. I hoped that I could meet her one day, especially as she would be as closely related to me as Sid, Christine and Barbara from my Mother Audrey's side.

We went to the churchyard and searched out all the family graves and walked again by the river. We visited places of interest, and walked through this homely, welcoming town again. We met friends and neighbours of the family, and people that knew Fred, and Ethel, his second wife. She had died a widow, having had happy years with him.

It was difficult, to leave this place, this Tref-y-Clawdd, Town on the Dyke, a town which spanned Wales and England, exactly as I did.

By the time we arrived home I felt utterly exhausted, both emotionally and physically.

Two weeks of non-stop driving, talking, listening, laughing and sometimes crying had taken its toll, but I wouldn't have missed any of it.

I now had to take stock of all that had happened, and report to our boys. A fortnight ago they had a mother with generations of history, and me, their father, with but sixty four years I could account for, and they had shared about half of that with me anyway. Things looked a little different now.

Two weeks after we returned to the Island from Wales, brother Sid came to visit us. He called me brother when we first met, as did Christine. They accepted me as an equal part of our Mother.
I felt that I belonged. We are now as close as any brother and sisters could be, so I have not referred to them as half siblings, which would be technically correct.

Throughout this narrative I have called them brother and sister, and equally Barbara in Australia. Likewise I refer to my Fathers daughter, Gwen. (Little Gwen)

Sid was able to tell me much more about our Mother. He was three years old when I was born, so didn't remember anything about it. He had been sent to Sheffield on the orders of his Father, and was not returned for a long time. Dated photographs show that he visited his Mother at Long Eaton in 1944, but he is uncertain when he returned to stay permanently, but was probably in time to start school. His father returned at about this time.

Sid sometimes visited a neighbours house to play table top snooker. One day, while there, from the window, Audrey was seen in her garden, heavily pregnant, this was just before Christine was born. 1946. The remark between the neighbours was,

"I wonder who's this one is"

Sid understood from that day what pregnancy meant. Not the best way to learn. It was an unfair comment to make about Audrey, as they would not have known anything about the circumstances leading up to my own birth, but were obviously aware of it.

Sid did not have a very good relationship with his father, who he didn't even know when he returned from the war.
Sid in his young years, was acting the man of the house, until this stranger appeared and took over.

Over the next few weeks I had many telephone calls from family members that I hadn't yet met. The families' grapevines had obviously been busy. I had to continually be checking my lists, in order not to make the mistake of putting the caller into the wrong family.

At Christmas time we received about ten times the greeting cards we normally received.

Auntie Dill phoned me on Christmas Day. She said that she was so pleased I had appeared. It was a bit of Fred come back.
She asked me to promise to come back to Knighton soon, so that she could tell me everything about my Father. There would be things that only she knew, being his little sister.

Also on Christmas Day I received a call from my sister Barbara in Australia.
It was quite a moment when she first spoke to me.
However it was not long before it seemed the most natural thing in the world to be having a conversation with her.
We both hoped that it might be possible to meet one day.
She had previously sent me a photograph of her and her husband Pete's family, a fine looking Aussie crowd.

New Year's Day brought my first family bad news. Auntie Dill had had a serious stroke and was in hospital in Hereford.

I had made her a promise, and I wasn't going to let her down.

A few days later I took the train to Ludlow, where it was convenient for Wally to meet me, and we drove to Hereford.
We found Auntie Dill in a bad way. She didn't know us.
It was a very sad start to a new year.

Wally had been in touch with Gwen, Fred's daughter, my sister, but I had heard nothing from her. Because of my experience the first time I had spoken to Christine, I knew it would be difficult. This time I was well aware that she actually was the person I wanted to speak to. I wanted more than that. I wanted my Father's daughter to be my sister, and I knew that she had been told about me. What I didn't know was whether or not she knew of me before Wally's call.

I had a lovely photograph beside me of Gwen as a young girl.
What a beautiful sister she was. Had we been brought up together, I'm sure that I would have looked after her.

I couldn't make the phone call.
I trembled at the thought of hearing her voice.

Once again my wife took over for me. Not so delicate a situation as with the first conversation with Christine, because Gwen did know about me.
The call was made.

The response was short and to the point.

"I think its all best left in the past" she said, and disconnected.

Perhaps I should have been prepared for this, but I was not. I was on such a high because of the way I had so far been received by all my new relations, that I didn't expect a rejection. I was very upset. I decided that I wouldn't give up. I couldn't. She was important to Fred, and she was now important to me. I would leave it a while and perhaps write her a letter.

Auntie Dill was in hospital for quite some time. She had been moved to another hospital nearer to Knighton. I visited her twice, and saw little improvement. While she was there her husband, Barbara's father, died. He was a nice man, and also was known as "Curly". I went to his funeral in St Edwards Church in Knighton. It was a good send off for a good old boy.

As happens at these sort of events, I was introduced to many family friends again. I was feeling like a local.

Auntie Dill was in hospital for some time. I visited her while she was there. She could not speak, but she held my hand and murmured. It was so pitiful to see her that way.
Eventually she returned home to her cottage, and was diligently looked after by her daughter Barbara. She passed away on July 31st 2008.

I went to her well-attended funeral in St Edwards Church, and said goodbye to her at Knighton Cemetery. She never was able to tell me everything about her favourite brother, my Father. It wouldn't surprise me if she got to tell him all about me.

I met several other, until then unknown, family members that day, including Bill, the cousin Wally mistook me for when I first phoned him. He was able to tell me more stories about Fred, my Father, and the jokes he used to play.
He later sent me a nice photograph of both our fathers together.

Fred with cousin Bill's Dad.
"All dressed up and nowhere to go"

Bill's father was a coach driver at Knighton.

He used to collect the coach from the garage and then call at his mother's for breakfast before picking up his trippers for the day.
One morning as he set off, he heard something in the back of the coach, and on inspection found Fred hiding. He was about twelve. Too late for school, trippers waiting, so Fred gets a day out and a return trip to Llandudno!

When Fred lived in Harrow, Bill used to skip off school to visit him. Fred was working shift work at Kodak. He was always good for fixing things, for instance a broken bicycle chain.
Not only would he mend the bike, he would give it a paint up as well. Bill always left in time to arrive home at the same time as if he had been to school. One day he was in trouble.
A neighbour had seen him near Fred's house, and reported Bill to his mother.

Bill became a heating engineer, and was one day installing a lengthy stainless steel chimney liner. He was up a ladder trying to push it down the chimney but it wouldn't go. It then started to go the wrong way. Looking down, Bill saw Fred hanging on the end. He had been driving past and saw Bill's van, so stopped for a bit of fun.

Eventually they both ended up on the ladder against the chimney, to get the job done.

By now, I had no doubt what waiting to do my search had cost me. I had missed my birth parents, and already within two years, I had attended two funerals amongst those I had found. I determined to make the most of being part of these two wonderful families.
We attended brother Sid's surprise 70th birthday party at Staverton Station in Devon, where he was a voluntary helper for some years with the South Devon Heritage Railway. Our sister Barbara was on a visit from Australia at the time, and I first met her there. Sid's son Andrew was also present, as was sister Christine and Bob, her husband. It was a great day. This was the first, and probably the only time, that I would be in the company of my siblings.

John, Barbara, Sid, Christine.
The first time our Mother's children had ever been together. August 23rd, 2009.

Sid and Barbara came over to the Island shortly afterwards, and we managed to get all our family, sons, daughters-in-law, partners and grand children all assembled for a party. It was time to let them know what I had brought with me when joining their family. Our family now, of course. Christine and Bob paid a visit every year, and several of the Knighton cousins, and second cousins, we have been pleased to welcome.

My family, as introduced to my new found families. 9th September. 2009.

It is the letters in my file which have given me more information than I ever hoped I would find.
It was a very emotional moment when first I saw my Mother's handwriting, and touched something she had touched.

The anguish felt by my Mother and her brother almost makes me feel guilty for being born, but the joy I brought to my Mum makes me glad that I was. I have had two sets of parents who, for good or bad, have contributed to make me who I am. I wonder what they would think of me, laying it all before whoever might be reading this now.

I am not attempting to generalise about adoption, or lay claim to knowing much about the current process. I am only telling my story as I understand it, from the actual facts. This is not a story made up of assumptions or hearsay. Unlike some authors, (not that I am one, I'm a retired boat builder), I haven't pretended that I remember every word spoken by every person mentioned, and I haven't flowered it up to make it more readable for those who enjoy a good story. What you are reading, if you are still there, is an accurate and true tale of an adopted child who found his birth families.

I hope that my story might give some understanding of how my adoption process worked. I hope that any adoptee reading this who is unable to have the good fortune to locate their file, might appreciate that there were people who cared. Whether it was a parent giving them up for the child's benefit, or an orphanage staffed by loyal helpers, there was always someone who cared.

I realise that I have been lucky, and that others may not have my good fortune, but if you were adopted, then you were given a second chance, and should be thankful for it.

Everyone has a right to know where they came from, and it is not easy for those adopted a long time ago to find out.
Were it not for the meticulous records kept by the National Children's Home, then I would never have known from where I came. I shall always be grateful to them.

I wish I had started my search a long time ago, although that is probably because it's been so successful. I might not have the same wish if it had proved a disaster.

I know now, of course, that all the information concerning my adoption was locked away at The National Children's Home. I could have found it at any time. It was just a phone call away. If it hadn't been for the clue of my Mum having supported them, I could have spent years getting nowhere. Apart from that, even if I had been able to search, there was no way of knowing what might be found.

I presume that most adoptees who know that they are adopted, but know nothing of their birth parents, experience times when their imaginations run riot. It didn't happen to me very often, but there were times when I wondered if I could possibly have been happier with my birth parents. These thoughts were generally after an argument, or friction with other family members, or when I had been punished for something, which was a rare occurrence. Rare, not because I was very good, but because I obeyed the rules, most of the time!

There was never any serious ill feeling towards my parents, however forceful the telling off or the clip around the ear. I am so thankful that although having my feelings hurt, I didn't ever remind my Mum and Dad that they were not my real parents. They didn't deserve that. They would have been heartbroken if I had taken that attitude.

I never ever considered that I wasn't "an Islander". When I applied for my first passport I entered my place of birth as Wootton Bridge, as it was the only place I thought I could put.
After all, I had always been there. It was evident from photographs of me before I could even sit up, grow hair, or have teeth. I didn't think I could ever have been anywhere else.
I was proud to be a "Caulk Head", as Islanders are known.
This was only until the time that my grandmother revealed the information about me, to my wife. I was a little disappointed, having then been told that I was a "Londoner".

My passport application was returned to me, with a note saying that Wootton Bridge was not recognised as a place of birth.
I returned the application form, with a note, saying that I could not claim anywhere else as a place of birth, owing to the fact that I had been adopted, and lived all my life there.

It seems that I am the only person in the world who was officially born at Wootton Bridge. It says so on my passport.

I would have liked to have found my birth families much earlier.
It would have been nice to have done things together with my brother, sisters and cousins, when we were all younger. As it is, none of us has the energy, or good enough health, to partake in the things we might have done years ago, with age on our side.
However, I'm sure we are making the best of what time is left to us.

It is unfortunate, though, that family members are passing on before I get to know them well. I don't think I would ever have known Gwen, my

Father's daughter, but I have missed all the stories that Auntie Dill, and Christine's husband Bob, who has now left us, could have told.

I don't think that my own children will ever be close to my found families. The distance in genes and generations is too wide and they have their own full lives to lead.

My Mum and Dad can just be remembered by some of my grandchildren, and are well, and affectionately remembered by our sons. My Mum and Dad will always be their grandparents, as far as they are concerned. That pleases me, as it confirms the fact that my adoption was a success, and adopted or not, we were, and are, a family.

I was extremely lucky that The National Children's Home still had my file after sixty four years. I might never have contacted them, had it not been for the clue left by my Mum, through her collections for them.

My search would have been easier, and probably earlier, if I had been told the truth. I don't know whether that would have been a good thing or not. My sister Christine thinks our Mother, would probably not have wanted to know me. Christine knew our Mother, I did not. Can a woman give birth and not want to know how the child fared in life?. My sister Barbara was born on the 10th April, 1948, the day before my sixth birthday. A painful reminder perhaps.

As for my Father, I have no idea . . . . Did he disappear when he realised his affair was going to produce a child, or was he in such a position that there was little he could do about it?
It is a natural thing for a man to want a son, a bit of himself, to set forth in the world and continue the family name. Men like to teach their sons not to make the same mistakes that they have.

Did Fred and Audrey ever think that they would bring me up together with her first born, believing that her husband would never return? Were they so ashamed that they wanted to be rid of the child and return to their pre-affair lives? It appears that they both lived full and happy lives without me . . . . without a thought of me, or even of each other perhaps.

These questions give me little bother. I had the very best up-bringing, by a Mum and Dad and grandparents who loved me as I loved them.

It is a fact that answers have only raised more questions. When I first wrote my notes after seeing my file, I thought I had most of the answers, but closer examination showed far more than I had realised. Letters which seemed insignificant at first held information which has given far more insight into what transpired all those years ago. I have a clear picture of what my Mother was going through, and of the great effort made by her brother. I also know my Mum's part, and I understand her better now than I ever did.

According to Fred Gammon's Army Service Record, 1940-1953, he was stationed at Derby in the first few years. His leave was spent between Long Eaton and Coventry, where one of his sisters lived. He was wounded and hospitalised three times during his service.

Interesting to me, is the fact that he was granted seven days leave (Long Eaton) August 1941, but was reprimanded for taking extra days (AWOL). This is the period in which I was conceived. Further leaves were taken at Long Eaton almost until the time of my birth, April 1942.

No leave seems to have been taken at his lodgings in Harrow, or at Knighton in Wales, the home of his mother and next of kin.

His next of kin was changed on the record in October, 1942, when he married Gwendoline, his land lady, who owned the Harrow house. Gwen, (Little Gwen), my sister, was born to them in November the following year, 1943. She passed away without ever meeting me, or replying to my letters. I will never know why she didn't want to know me, or whether she knew about me before Wally's phone call to her in November 2006.

It seems logical that Fred knew Audrey was pregnant, and also that I had been born, because of the times he spent at Long Eaton in 1941/2. Audrey had little alternative, other than to give me up, having learnt that her husband would eventually be returning from war. This probably became apparent at a late stage of her pregnancy which was when she sought help from her brother Raymond Ashmore. Whether it was his idea that I should be disposed of in the manner he first attempted, or Audry's, I will never know.

The situation for my Mother was desperate, having had her other son taken from her. I wish though that adoption had been the first choice. It could not be known that my adoption would be as successful as it was, but surely better to be in family home than an orphanage.

I am glad for Audrey's sake, and for my sister's, that her husband returned from war, and can only speculate as to any other outcome.

Fred was in no position to do anything except, perhaps, to assist with the payments towards my care. However at the time, he was in debt to the Army Paymaster, although it had been requested by his Major, that the debt be wiped off.
This was confirmed in one of Raymond Ashmore's letters.
The request could only have been instigated by the debtor himself of course. I would like to think that Fred was willing, and had full intentions of assisting, but was unable. I shall never know the true facts.

Audrey's husband was informed of her affair by one of his sisters. Another sister vaguely remembered the arguments between them at the time, and relayed the information to my sister, at the time I found the Hayler family. My brother Sid knew a little about this from his cousin, a daughter of one of the sisters, with whom he spent some time as a child. The interference of the sisters, caused a lasting family rift.

On receiving the news of Audrey's pregnancy, her husband commenced divorce proceedings, and had their first born son removed from Audrey. He subsequently offered to halt the divorce and allow their son to return to his mother, provided I was disposed of at birth. This is probably why Raymond Ashmore asked the Home to take me directly I was born. This was not possible as babies could not be accepted for at least four weeks after birth. Even then, should I have proved unsuitable to my adopters, or been of ill health, then I would have been returned to my Mother.

Closer examination of my file revealed a few inaccuracies in the notes made of my meeting at Horsham. I now have a clearer picture of the happenings leading to my adoption, and the event itself. The true facts have been gleaned mostly from the various letters between all parties concerned.

My Mum had a hysterectomy in Guy's hospital in London in 1937. She was twenty two years old. This was a complicated operation at that time. She and my Dad had been going together for some time before this. In the full knowledge that they could not produce a child between them, they nevertheless married in 1939. Adoption was a consideration, as their was some experience of adoption in my Mum's family.

At the beginning of 1942 they applied to the National Children's Home to enquire about adopting a baby boy. They were told that they would be considered.

Raymond Ashmore first contacted the National Children's Home, by letter, wrongly dated April 12th, 1941.

John Sheen

The Matron,
National Children's Home.
Alexandra Park. Notts.
                                      Barnsley Road,
                                                Fir Vale.
                                              Sheffield.5.
                                                12/4/41.

Dear Matron,

    I am seeking information with regard to the placing of a baby into a Home and shall be ever thankful if you can help and guide in this matter. The baby will be born on Tues or Wed, April 14/15 in a Derby Maternity Home, and I wish to know if you can accept the baby into your Home direct from the Maternity Home, when the mother is allowed to come out. The father of the baby is a soldier, my Sister is the mother who lives in Notts, and has been so ashamed of her condition that she has just written to me for help.

    I have written to the soldier's C.O. and he is making arrangements with the Army Paymaster regarding allocation of pay.

I will give you all the information for the Completion of Records if you will reply by return to say that you will accept the baby direct from the Maternity Home and so enable me to place my Sister's miserable mind at rest over the child's welfare. The Commanding Officer of the Soldier's Unit, has, since I first wrote to him on March 17th, been trying to arrange for the new-born child to enter the Army Foundling Home but the difficulty appears to be that my Sister is not in the Services yet, although they may waive the point and give their authority later for the child to enter. This does not solve my immediate difficulty of disposing of the baby direct from the Home, to allow my Sister to get back to her responsibilities, and I shall be forever grateful if you can offer your own solution in this world of private trouble.

Yours truly,
    Raymond Ashmore.

The above letter is misdated by one year. Perhaps reflecting the strain the writer was under. At this stage, having me adopted hadn't been considered. The problem was "Disposing of the baby". There was no mention of adoption, just "the placing of the baby into a Home" be it The Army Foundling Home, or The National Children's Home.

Adoption was suggested by The National Children's Home in their letter of 15th April, as I would then, most likely, only be accommodated quickly, and for a short period. The suggestion seems to have been readily accepted by Raymond Ashmore, although it did not offer immediate disposal, as hoped for, and there would be some responsibilities.

John Sheen

NATIONAL CHILDREN'S HOME

15th April, 1942.

C/MP.
Mr R. Ashmore.
Barnsley Road,
Fir Vale,
Sheffield. 5.

Dear Sir,

It is a little difficult to make firm promises with regard to an unborn child.
If the suggestion is that the child should Remain in our care, then application should be made after the birth, and whether we could receive the child or nor would depend on the circumstances and the vacancies at that time.

If the mother is willing for adoption into some well selected home, then it would be highly probable that we should receive the baby, because it would not be in our care very long. In that case everything would depend upon the physical perfection of the child.

We should be happy to hear from you again after the baby is born, and to give our most careful and sympathetic consideration.
We regret that we cannot take the child direct from the maternity home if adoption is required.

Yours faithfully,

Well Worth Waiting For

Barnsley Road,
Fir Vale, Sheffield. 5.
19/4/42

Dear Sirs,

I thank you for your letter dated 15/4/42 ref: C/MP and appreciate your kindness in the matter and assure you of my speedy co-operation to settle this disgusting upheaval. I have visited your District Representative and Advocate, Mr and Mrs Schofield of Creswick Greave, Grenoside, Nr Sheffield, and they gave me every consideration and advised me to make arrangements with you direct.

The Child was born on April 11th, and is a boy weighing 7lbs 9ozs and my Sister would be able to part with this baby within 4 weeks after coming from the Maternity Home and then she would be able to receive her own son back from his enforced stay in Sheffield. My Sister will be discharged from the Nightingale Home on Thursday next 23rd, and I have asked her to obtain the Doctor's Certificate showing the baby's state of health.

It is most important that this baby is placed in good care with the least possible delay, and if adoption cannot take effect within the next 4 weeks, can you receive the baby earlier than this as the husband, who is a Prisoner of War, has, in view of the circumstances which brought about the baby's existence, forgiven my Sister providing she parts with the baby at the earliest possible moment in order that her own son may come home. The father of the baby is Gunner F. R. Gammon No 999521 of 120th A.A. "Z" Battery R A. H.Q. Staff 149 Warwick Road, Coventry and his home address is 29, Stanley Road, South Harrow, Middx. He is 28 years of age and I have written to his Major Commanding regarding maintenance pay, and he informs me that Gnr Gammon is at present in debt with Army Pay

Office and the Major is trying to get it wiped out with the Paymaster.

If this is not successful, my Sister will commence weekly payments now for the baby's keep. How much will this amount to please.

Is it correct to Christen the baby with the father's Surname.

Kindly give this matter your careful consideration as I am at a loss as to where to turn if you cannot receive the baby.

Thanking you,
   Yours truly,
     Raymond Ashmore.

NATIONAL CHILDREN'S HOME

MEC/E   23rd April, 1942

Mr R. Ashmore.

Barnsley Road,
Fir Vale.
Sheffield. 5.

Dear Mr Ashmore,
   In reply to your letter of the 19th inst. Will you please have the enclosed form completed and returned to us, and the Medical Form of course, having to be filled in by a doctor.
I am sorry we cannot promise to receive the little one within the next four weeks as the accommodation at our Babies Home is full, and I hope it will be possible for some interim arrangement to be made for the little one until he can come to us. The unfortunate position is that practically all applications for the reception of babies are for baby boys, where as adopters, want baby girls, and consequently we are unable to move as quickly as we should.

Certainly we will do our best to expedite matter for receiving the little one, and hope before too long a good adoption should be effected. The adoption will however, in all probability take some time, but we shall not delay on this account.

                                         Yours sincerely,

John Sheen

NATIONAL CHILDREN'S HOME

MEC/E   19th May, 1942

Mr R. Ashmore.
Barnsley Road,
Fir Vale.
Sheffield. 5.

Dear Mr. Ashmore,
           Re: Harold Hayler.

   Many thanks for the completed forms.

At the moment the accommodation at our Adoption Babies Home is full, but we will receive this little one as soon as possible, and hope the mother will take him to Harpenden.

   When writing, giving the date for his reception, we will send directions for getting to our Babies Home there, also a list of articles which should be taken with the little one, or anyhow as many as possible.

   With many thanks,

           Yours sincerely,

The Secretary.　　　　　　　　　## Barnsley Road,
National Children's Home　　　　　　　Fir Vale,
　　　　　　　　　　　　　　　　　　Sheffield.
　　　　　　　　　　　　　　　　May 21st / 42

Dear Mrs Crutcher,
Many thanks for your very welcome letter of 19th inst, advising me of your acceptance of this dear baby, Harold Hayler, into your Home at the earliest future date.
I fully appreciate the valuable help you have given to me in this disgusting case under Wartime Conditions and I will gladly subscribe to your cause when War Emergency calls against income ease off to a more peaceful-like stability. I am expecting to be called to the Services in the near future as my deferment time expires, but will certainly make every endeavour to contribute to the Home's income, however small my effort may be.
With Best Wishes, Yours sincerely
　　　　　　　R Ashmore.

The National Children's Home, having offered a place in their Babies Home, which was full at the time, didn't deter Raymond Ashmore from trying to get me, or as I was referred to, "It", accommodated somewhere, in the mean time. I was obviously still with my Mother at that time. 12th June, 1942

I was taken to Akrill House, the Babies Home at Harpenden on 15th July 1942. Not by my Mother, but by a Social Worker.
I had spent a month in a foster home.

Akrill House

Akrill House was built in 1897 to the design of architect Robert William Edis, at the behest of Sir John Blundell Maple M.P. (1845-1903) of Childwickbury. Its purpose was to serve as a convalescent home for sick employees in the London furniture firm bearing his name. He also commissioned the building nearby of a similarly styled group of Almshouses for his retired employees, and provided an endowment for their up-keep. The Hertfordshire Mercury, of 12th June 1897, described Akrill House as "of Elizabethan style, on high ground to the north of Harpenden, with ground floor accommodation for twelve women, a steward and matron, with a well furnished sitting room for those whose case may require perfect quietude and rest". Such was the concern of Sir John for his employees, a philanthropic ethos not uncommon among wealthy Victorians.
The building acquired its name of Akrill House, owing to a bequest from Mrs Elizabeth Akrill, wife of Charles Akrill (1840-1907).

She left the sum of ten thousand pounds to purchase land and build within two years of her death a convalescent home for women and children, or a home for crippled children. The site was to be either in Worcestershire or North Wales, "or elsewhere as my trustees may decide". The trustees decided that in conjunction with the National Children's Home, already based in Harpenden, Mrs Akrill's wishes could be met. Akrill house was subsequently transferred to sole National Children's Home ownership. As time passed, the mode of use of Akrill House changed, first to an adoption centre for babies, and for training girls in their care. From 1946-1997 it then served as a house for the retired Sisters, who had worked in their service, principally at Highfield Oval. In 1982 National Children's Home and a local builder, Tomblin and Sons, were granted planning permission to convert Akrill House into seven flats and the building of a block of twelve flats in what had been the garden, The work was completed in 1983. The building still stands as a memorial to its benefactors, Sir John Blundell Maple and Mrs Elizabeth Akrill.

Extracts from Harpenden Local History Society, by Audrey Deacon.

My Mum received a letter dated 5th August 1942, asking if she would care to consider a three month old baby boy. It stated that "he is a fine little chap, and his Medical Certificate is excellent. He is named Harold Hayler. Born April 11th 1942". Known details of the mother were given, but very sparse information about the father. The mother's brother had introduced the case, supported by voluntary workers living in the area.

There is a typing error in the letter. The baby's name is given as Harold Hayler in the subject matter, but he is called John within the letter itself. Quite a coincidence.
I wonder if that is where my Mum got the idea to name me.

John Sheen

NATIONAL CHILDREN'S HOME.

MEC/G.   5th August 1942.

Mrs S. Sheen.
"Glenholme"
New Road,
Wootton Bridge.
Isle of Wight.

Dear Mrs Sheen,
<ins>re: Harold Hayler.</ins>

We think you may care to consider the above-named who was born April 11, 1942, at Derby.

The mother, aged twenty-eight, is married. According to the facts given to us in the application, her husband is a prisoner of war, and has forgiven her. There is a little boy of the marriage. The father of the illegitimate little one is a gunner on active service, and aged twenty-nine, but we have not been informed whether he is a married man or not. Any further information on such points as you may desire, we will ascertain as far as possible. The case was introduced to us by the mother's brother, and supported by some of our voluntary workers of long standing, also the Secretary of the local branch of the Charity Organisation Society, living in the same district as the mother.

John was received at Harpenden on July 15th 1942, the mother having given her written Consent to Adoption on May 11, 1942. The little boy is a fine little chap, and ready for adoption. His Medical Certificate is excellent. I am sorry I cannot give details of his appearance, as I have not yet seen him, but shall be doling so at the weekend I expect.

As, however, it is essential we effect adoptions without delay, both to create vacancies as quickly as possible and to meet the wishes of adopters, we should likr you to have the opportunity of considering Harold now.
   Thanking you,
      Yours sincerely,

My Mum replied that she and my Dad were definitely interested, and requested further information, particularly about the father.

There was little to go on except that the mother, through her brother, had stated "he was very healthy, of average intelligence, a romancer, and always polite. He had done numerous jobs for local residents and certainly had winning ways with him. His mother, a widow, lives in Knighton in Wales. He was a painter and decorator by trade." The mother's brother had never met him.

In reply to the enquiry about the baby's father, the mother's brother had added his own thoughts. "If Harold had been God's gift under normal circumstances, I would not be writing this now, and my constant prayer is that, with God's guidance, Harold will not bear any resemblance to his father, or develop his unclean mind".

He further states, "He was a painter and decorator by trade, like Hitler, and as befits all wrong doers, will probably meet an appropriate end". This part of the letter was not passed on to my Mum. The original was still in my file.

Raymond Ashmore first wrote to The National Children's Home on 12th of April, the day after I was born, stating that the birth was expected on 14th or 15th. He stated that his sister had just recently written to him for help. He had also attempted to get the baby placed in the Army Foundling Home, but this was not possible as his sister was not in the services but, exceptionally, they may waive the point because the father was. This was a very unusual offer by the Army. Only orphans of married service couples would normally be considered for acceptance.

This, however was not a solution to the immediate problem.

It is not clear why my Mother waited so long to seek help.

My brother Sid knows that there were three telegrams informing our Mother of her husband's whereabouts. He strongly feels that one of the telegrams was the dreaded "Missing in action, presumed dead", and that the news of his father's imprisonment came at a late stage in her pregnancy. It is known that our Mother's husband was going to divorce her, but subsequently offered to withdraw proceedings provided the baby was given up at birth. Her first born, Sid, who had been taken away by his father's family would then be returned to her.

It seems that it was at this time Raymond Ashmore was approached for help. My father, Fred Gammon, was a single man, serving in the Army, in the middle of a world war. He could not be responsible for me, even if he had wanted to be.

The Home wrote to Raymond Ashmore on July 6th, saying that they were now ready to accept the baby, and requesting the mother to take him to Akrill House at Harpenden. Precise directions were given for the train journey via Kings Cross and St Pancras stations. The journey time should be about one hour.

There was a list of items required for the baby, together with the forms re. diet and freedom from infection, which must be completed.

Wherever possible, the Adoption Committee expected a small regular contribution towards the baby's maintenance until adoption was established. The improbability of the mother being able to make any payments had been noted on a previous form, but she could not be released from all responsibility in that way, and a reply on this point was requested.

In reply to Raymond Ashmore's concern about what would happen to the child should the adoption not proceed, he was told the baby would certainly be returned to his mother.

A letter from the Derby Charity Organisation Society to The Adoption Home, dated July 17th, refers to the baby being taken to Akrill House on the previous Wednesday 15th, by a Mrs Woolley. She had spoken to Audrey about contributions while the baby was awaiting adoption. Apparently she had been paying twelve shillings per week to a foster mother, but it had caused hardship. She now offered to pay two shillings and sixpence to the Home. I was at the foster mother's for four weeks.

A letter from the Home to Mrs Woolley on 4th August states that there has been no response regarding contributions, and that they were again writing to Mr Ashmore.

They had in view a prospective adoption home, but were at the moment in preliminary correspondence, and did not know if it would materialise.

On 6th August the Home wrote to Raymond Ashmore regarding prospective adopters, but pointing out that no contributions had been received.

118

NATIONAL CHILDREN'S HOME AND ORPHANAGE
HIGHBURY PARK, LONDON, N.5

August 11, 1948.

I, AUDREY KAYLER hereby agree to pay to the Rev. John H. Litten, or other the Principal for the time being, of the NATIONAL CHILDREN'S HOME AND ORPHANAGE, Highbury Park, London, N.5, the sum of Five shillings per week in consideration of the reception into the said NATIONAL CHILDREN'S HOME AND ORPHANAGE of HAROLD KAYLER

The said payments shall be made in regular monthly (calendar) instalments of £ 1. 1. 0. the first thereof to be made on the 15th day of August and shall so continue as long as the said until three months after adoption transfer has been effected. remains in the Principal's care. If at any time there shall be more than four weeks in arrears, I will, on receiving notice to remove the child, undertake to provide for such removal within the space of fourteen days after receiving notice, the said removal to be at my own expense in all things.

Signed Audrey Kayler

Address 6, Ray Lane
Long Eaton
Nr Nottingham

Witness R W Bentley
Address "Elwyn" Hope Lane
Long Eaton.

Harold Hayler had been brought to the attention of my eventual adoptive Mum and Dad by letter, on 5th August 1942.
Details of my Mother and her situation were given, including that her husband was a prisoner of war. It was stated that the father of the illegitimate child was on active service, but it was not know if he was married. The case had been introduced by the mother's brother, supported by some of their voluntary workers, and the Secretary of the local branch of the Charity Organisation Society.

The letter stated that JOHN had been received at Harpenden on July 15th, the mother having given written consent to adoption on May 11th. The boy was a "fine little chap" and ready for adoption. His Medical Record was excellent.

My Mum replied that she felt interested in Harold Hayler, but would like to know more about his appearance, as she wanted a fair child.

My Mum received two letters sent 11th August, asking if she would like to make an early appointment to visit Harpenden and receive Harold, should she decide on trial adoption.

The Home needed vacancies badly, and had many adopters looking for baby boys, but were offering the first opportunity in this case to her. This is the complete opposite of what Raymond Ashmore had been told, which was that most adopters wanted girls.

The second letter was an enclosure that said that the writer had been at the Babies' Home over the weekend, and had seen Harold. "He is a dear little boy whom one cannot fail to love, and he is fair in colouring, with clear skin, and is bonny altogether"

My Mum replied that she didn't think that she could make the return journey from the Isle of Wight within a day, but would check ferry and train times. It was arranged to bring the baby to Waterloo Station on August 20th.

Wootton Bridge
I. of. Wight

Dear Miss Crutcher,

re. Harold Hayler

I thank you for your letter of the 14th inst.

It would be a great help to me to be able to meet Harold at Waterloo as you suggest, Thursday 30th would be the most convenient day for me.

I think it would be better to say that we would meet in the Ladies' waiting room at Waterloo Station, as my train arrives soon after 10 o'clock, I will wait there.

I shall be wearing a yellow coat and brown felt hat.

Yours sincerely
Maud Skeen

John Sheen

NATIONAL CHILDREN'S HOME.

MEC/E.   17th August, 1942

MRS S SHEEN.
"Glenholme"
New Road,
Wootton Bridge.
Isle of Wight.

Dear Mrs Sheen,

<u>Re: Harold Hayler.</u>

Thank you for your letter at hand this morning.

    Yes, our worker will bring Harold to the Ladies Waiting Room at Waterloo Station on Thursday next, the 20th inst.
Thank you for telling us what you will be wearing.

We know you will kindly send us a letter to tell us of your safe arrival home.

    Many thanks,

                                           Yours sincerely,

It had been pointed out to Raymond Ashmore that before anything was done to bring Harold to the attention of the prospective adopters, the Adoption Committee needed a reply to previous correspondence. This related to contributions for the three months from the date the transfer was actually effected. This was a statutory period prior to final adoption.

An urgent reply was needed because this opportunity for Harold may be lost, and another opportunity may not be forthcoming for some time, most adoption proposals being for baby girls.

A letter dated 11th August from National Children's Home in connection with payment, said that the mother's brother had sent on a letter he had received from Mrs Woolley of the C.O.S. who had brought Harold to Akrill House. In the letter was the following paragraph.
"The home is a delightful place, and although I saw Mrs Hayler's home and saw that she was indeed a very good mother, the child could never have had such good care as he will get now. The surroundings are lovely in every way, and the children could not be more beautifully kept, and cared for if they were in a Royal Nursery. There is no hint of an orphanage or institution as most people understand it. This particular home is a very nice private house, in a lovely garden".

A further letter of the same date, 11th August, was sent to Raymond Ashmore reporting that Harold had been brought to the notice of potential adopters, who wanted to know if there was any possibility of knowing more about the father.
He was also asked if it would be convenient for him and the mother jointly, to pay five shillings per week in order to satisfy The Adoption Committee's rule.

On 14th August Akrill House were given the details of the prospective adopters. Mrs Tripp would handle the transfer, and would come to Harpenden for the child. It was suggested that he be handed over by the engine of the Portsmouth train at Waterloo Station, but the adopters had said that they would prefer to meet in the ladies' waiting room. This was agreed.

On 21st August my Mum wrote to advise of a safe journey home, and to say that she was delighted with the little boy.

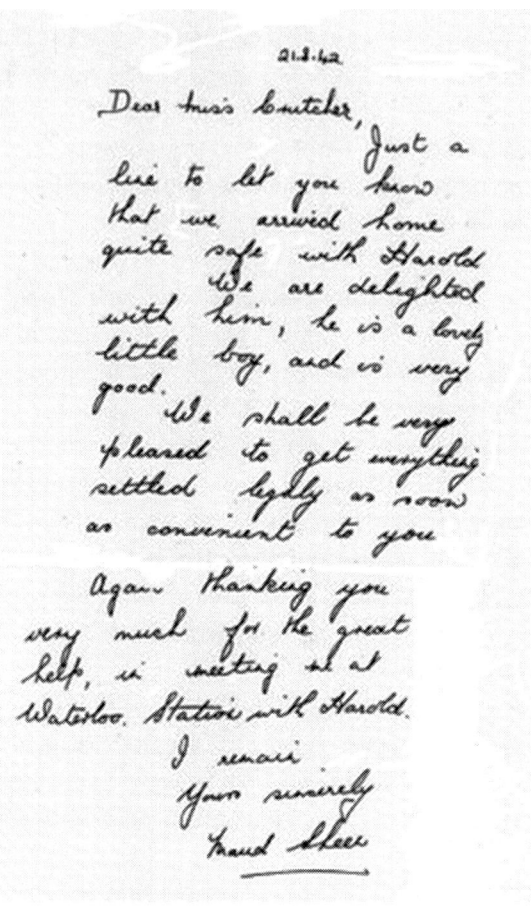

On 21st August Raymond Ashmore was informed that Harold went to his adoption home on the previous day. A successful permanent arrangement was anticipated, although there was no commitment, and it was entirely provisional.

He was again asked for a reply to two previous letters which had raised important matters, and needed attention.

Letters had crossed in the post, and a Postal Order to the value of one pound, one shilling and eight pence, was received, from Mr Ashmore, with a note that the next payment would be made on September 15th. He hoped the prospective adopters were still interested in Harold, and that they would in the near future decide to adopt him.

The Home wrote to Raymond Ashmore on 22nd September asking that the enclosed Consent and Declaration be signed by the mother in the presence of a Magistrate. He was told that the adopters were delighted with Harold, and that he was happily settled and gaining weight. They were now proceeding to legal formalities.

The Home wrote to Mrs Woolley, of Derby Charity Organisation Society, on 25th September regarding the baby's personal ration book, as it had not been handed over with him.

Mrs Woolley replied that she had written to Mrs Hayler, and to Mrs Ault, the foster mother, and had not received a reply from either of them. She could, however, not see that the adopters were being inconvenienced, because the baby was only just five months old and should not be The request had been misunderstood. It was the clothing coupons that were required, not sweets.

On October 13th, The Charity Organisation Society reported that they had received a reply from Mrs Hayler, who had not been able to find the ration book. She was certain that it had been handed over. She remembered that there was no name on the book. She apologised for not yet returning the Adoption Form, and said that she would go to see a Magistrate as soon as she felt better, and get it witnessed. She hoped she had not caused any inconvenience to Mr and Mrs Sheen, the adopters.

It seems strange that my Mother left it so long to visit the Magistrate, who, according to Sid my brother, lived a few yards away, in Dove Lane. Almost her next door neighbour!.

This was the final Document to legalise the adoption.

A letter to request that the parents should not be told of my adopters' name or address, infers that it was not known if my Father had been consulted, or was party to the adoption arrangements. The required forms had only been completed by my Mother.

When this was realised, my Mum must have lived in fear of a Welshman knocking on the door one day.

Well Worth Waiting For

Copy letter. Original faded.

New Road,
Wootton Bridge
Isle of Wight.

Dear Mrs Crutcher,
10/9/42

I am forwarding the forms of Application and Consent of Adoption of Harold Hayler, in future to be known as John Anthony Sheen. We should be very grateful if you would help us to fill in the necessary information, also we should be very glad if possible for the parents to fill in their part before us, as we would like to keep our address unknown to them.

Also will you kindly obtain the large birth certificate as required by the Court. We are glad to say that John is very happy, and his weight today was 16lb 5oz.

Will you please let me have his personal ration book also he should have the extra clothing coupons for use after October. I have used all of our own coupons on him. I enquired at the Local Office and they told me they were issued with his clothing book.

I hope we are not putting you to too much trouble, but it is all very strange to us, and we should be so glad to get it all settled.

Yours sincerely, Maud Sheen.

In a letter to Raymond Ashmore telling of my successful adoption, my progress to date was given. It was also said that they, either the Home or the writer, Mrs Crutcher, would be pleased to convey any further news received. I know that my new name of John had been made known, also my new surname. Raymond Ashmore had replied that they, presumably he and Audrey liked my new name, and were glad that I was happy.

My Mum regularly wrote to Mrs Crutcher giving details of my appearance and weight etc, my first haircut, (I had blonde curls, and was called "Bubbles" by some, not "Curly" like Fred Gammon, or Auntie Dill's husband), and relayed the fact that I was very interested in boats. I had won a prize at Sunday School for attendance and good conduct, and a prize at day school. I was also full of fun and could amuse myself entirely on my own. I spent hours just watching boats on the river. I could row a boat aged six, and made model ones too. All this was passed on. These reports continued until I was seven years old. There are none in my file from a later date than February 1949.

I questioned at my interview at Horsham, when I found out who I was, whether my Mother might have had any knowledge of my progress after adoption. I was told that it was not probable. My Mother should not have even known my new name or indeed the name of my adoptive parents. She did, of course. In fact my Mum was told that she would know.

> L Dove Lane
> Long Eaton
> Notts
>
> Oct 7"/43
>
> Miss Crutcher,
> Dear Madam,
>   I am very sorry I am at present unable to return Adoption Form for Baby Harold Bayler, owing to my own illness. As soon as I possibly can I will go to see a magistrate to get the form signed and witnessed. I hope this will not cause any inconvenience either to you or to Mr & Mrs Sheen.
>   May I take this opportunity to thank you for the attention and kindness you have given in the matter, I remain,
>   Yours very faithfully
>   Audrey A. Bayler.

I can't say that I ever spent a great deal of time thinking about my birth parents. but there were times in my life when I wondered what they might have thought of me, if they could have seen me breaking the 220yd record for under 13's at the Island School Athletic Championships, or passing my driving test on my scooter, first time, and similar things that were important to me.

I thought of them particularly when I was getting married, and when our first son was born. Their grandchild! Would Fred Gammon have gone up the road shouting out his name and weight, like my Dad did? I had no idea.

I'll never know if they missed me, or even if they ever thought of me.

10.9.43.   J.S.

Dear Mrs Crutchley,

I thought you would be pleased to know that John is making good progress, he is now running about & has 8 teeth; when I had him weighed about a month ago he was 26½ lbs. He has been perfectly well all the time; he is now having a course of injections against Diptheria & Whooping Cough.

He is a fine boy and is a very happy baby. We all love him very much and are very happy with him.

I Remain

Yours sincerely,

Maud Sheen

"Glenholme"
Hew Road
Wootton Bridge
I. of Wight

22.2.49.

Dear Mrs Loveday,

I thought you would like to know that John is progressing well. He is a fine little boy & very lovable, we can't imagine what it would be like without him now, we love him so much.

He is getting on nicely at school & had the prize in his class last year, and also Sunday school prize for good conduct, and I am sure you he is very proud of them.

In spite of all the sickness about at this time of the year, he has kept perfectly fit, for which we are very thankful.

He is full of life & fun, & can amuse himself playing all sorts of games on his own, he loves playing shops with us, he gets on well with other children.

With kindest regards & very best wishes,

Yours sincerely
Maud Shaw

My Mum with her dog "Floss"
Me with my Dad, 4 months old

Me with the train my Dad made for me.

With my Grandad and Great Grandparents

Me with our dog "Sally"

Frederick Roger Gammon
My Father.
1913-1984

Audrey Helen Hayler
My Mother.
1913-1997

Frederick Gammon and Audrey Hayler.

Summing up.

My story began over seventy years ago, and I realise that the adoption process has changed considerably in that time. Furthermore I was adopted during a world war, when it was probably deemed best to re-home the many wartime babies as quickly as possible. This, however, depended upon the adopters being suitable. There was not the amount of red tape, nor the checks which are considered absolutely necessary nowadays.

I honestly wonder whether better matches are made as a result.

Years ago official adoptions were in the majority, arranged by Christian organisations like The National Children's Home.
They, and the social workers involved, were generally in their occupation as a calling, not just as paid employees. The Sisters at The National Children's Home strived, through the care they showed, to attain a promotion from the Blue Badge to a Red. Badge, which was only obtained after twenty one years of service.

I can only speak of my own first hand experience, but I do know of others who experienced personal trauma through being adopted. It concerns me that what is today considered acceptable, can for some, lead to misery.

A child needs, and has a right, to have a Mother and a Father, be they biological or adopted.

Had I not had both in my adoptive parents, then I am certain that I should have been terribly confused, and lacking in my understanding of what life is. It is the product of Man + Woman. There is only one way.

We are taught that a family is a Mum and a Dad and their child or children. It is my belief that adopters should provide this.
I accept that it doesn't always work out, and that relationships breakdown, and children get left with one or other single parent.
However, the most important time is the start of a family, when children are so impressionable, when they are beginning to learn what makes them and their family. Easy for me to talk, I know. I was extremely lucky to be adopted by my Mum and Dad, and I hope I managed to show my appreciation to them. I would have been a different person without guidance from both of them

THE END

Lightning Source UK Ltd.
Milton Keynes UK
UKOW03f2245280414

230744UK00001B/2/P